THE OPEN

148TH ROYAL PORTRUSH

Aurum
Press

R&A

Aurum Press
74-77 White Lion Street, London N1 9PF

Published 2019 by Aurum Press

Copyright 2019 R&A Championships Limited

Course illustration by Strokesaver

Project coordinator: Sarah Wooldridge
Additional thanks to:
NTT Data
Peter Kollmann

A CIP catalogue record for this book is available
from the British Library

ISBN-13: 978-0-7112-5285-1

Designed and produced by Davis Design
Colour retouching by Luciano Retouching Services, Inc.
Printed in Italy by L.E.G.O.

THE OPEN

148TH ROYAL PORTRUSH

EDITOR
Andy Farrell

WRITERS AND PHOTOGRAPHERS

Writers	The R&A	Getty Images	Golf Editors
Peter Dixon	Ross Kinnaird	Andrew Redington	Cliff Hawkins
Andy Farrell	Warren Little	Stuart Franklin	Naomi Baker
John Hopkins	Richard Heathcote	Francois Nel	Mark Trowbridge
Lewine Mair	Matt Lewis	Kevin Cox	Linnea Rheborg
Philip Reid	Jan Kruger	Mike Ehrmann	Andy Smith
Art Spander	Tom Dulat	David Cannon	Kate McShane
Alistair Tait	Charles McQuillan	Luke Walker	

Foreword

By Shane Lowry

Even now I don't think it has sunk in properly but every time I look at the Claret Jug I smile and remember the greatest week of my life at The 148th Open at Royal Portrush.

It was always about The Open for me. I grew up back home at Esker Hills holing putts to win The Open. I watched Padraig Harrington win his two Opens. I didn't even know him back then and now we are very good friends. You go round to Paddy's house and the Claret Jug is sitting on the kitchen table — now it's sitting on my kitchen table too!

To my parents, I can't thank you enough for all the sacrifices you made for me when I was younger. To my wife Wendy and daughter Iris, just knowing you are there for me whatever I score has made a massive difference. And to my team, especially caddie Brian "Bo" Martin and coach Neil Manchip, you all believed I was good enough to win a major and that helped an awful lot.

Congratulations to everyone at Royal Portrush Golf Club, The R&A and all the local authorities who made the return of The Open to Northern Ireland such an incredible success. It's the best Open I've played in and the triumph was all yours.

Most importantly, thank you to all the fans who supported all the players so warmly and me so loudly. Those roars are still ringing in my ears! It's funny, sometimes in the past I struggled to play in front of a home crowd but not that week. It was a surreal experience listening to so many people chanting my name and something I will never, ever forget.

The R&A
Open Championships Committee

CHAIRMAN
Clive T Brown

COMMITTEE
Will Bailey
John Clark
Pat Crowson
Paul McKellar
David Meacher
Anne O'Sullivan

CHIEF EXECUTIVE
Martin Slumbers

EXECUTIVE DIRECTOR – CHAMPIONSHIPS
Johnnie Cole-Hamilton

EXECUTIVE DIRECTOR – GOVERNANCE
David Rickman

Introduction

By Clive T Brown,
Chairman, Open Championships Committee

The 148th Open at Royal Portrush will be remembered for a brilliant performance by Ireland's Shane Lowry, who lifted the famous Claret Jug for the first time after a six-stroke victory over Tommy Fleetwood.

On his way to becoming the 2019 Champion Golfer of the Year, Lowry set a new course record for the revised Dunluce Links with a magnificent 63 during the third round and he was only a whisker away from matching the low round record of 62 for a major championship set by Branden Grace at Royal Birkdale in 2017.

We enjoyed a truly special and historic week as The Open returned to Northern Ireland for the first time in nearly 70 years. The energy, celebration, emotion and passion of the crowd was remarkable and the dramatic scenes we saw will live long in the memories of those who were lucky enough to be there, as well as the millions of viewers watching on TV around the world.

With the help of Royal Portrush Golf Club and the local government agencies we staged the biggest sporting event ever to be held in Northern Ireland and achieved a record attendance for The Open outside St Andrews of 237,750 fans. I would like to thank them all for the years of hard work and planning that went into delivering a world class sporting event and experience for everyone who attended.

I also wish to thank the members and staff of Royal Portrush Golf Club and the thousands of volunteers who worked tirelessly before and during the Championship to ensure its smooth running.

The 148th Open was my last as Chairman of the Open Championships Committee and I wish my successor David Meacher the very best as we now look forward to The 149th Open at Royal St George's.

Adam Hadwin

Andrew Johnston

Graeme McDowell

Oliver Wilson

148TH ROYAL PORTRUSH

CANADA

RBC Canadian Open 6-9 June
Adam Hadwin, Canada
Graeme McDowell, Northern Ireland

USA

Arnold Palmer Invitational 7-10 March
presented by MasterCard
Sungjae Im, Korea
Sung Kang, Korea
Keith Mitchell, USA

Rocket Mortgage Classic 27-30 June
Nate Lashley, USA
Doc Redman, USA

John Deere Classic 11-14 July
Dylan Frittelli, South Africa

THE OPEN
QUALIFYING SERIES

SOUTH AFRICA

South African Open 6-9 December 2018
Romain Langasque, France
Oliver Wilson, England
Charl Schwartzel, South Africa

Jazz Janewattananond

Chan Kim

Nino Bertasio

Dylan Frittelli

EUROPE

Estrella Damm N.A. 27-30 June
**Andalucia Masters hosted by
the Sergio Garcia Foundation**
Christiaan Bezuidenhout, South Africa
Adri Arnaus, Spain
Mike Lorenzo-Vera, France

Dubai Duty Free Irish Open 4-7 July
Bernd Wiesberger, Austria
Robert Rock, England
Paul Waring, England

**Aberdeen Standard Investments
Scottish Open** 11-14 July
Benjamin Hebert, France
Andrew Johnston, England
Nino Bertasio, Italy

FINAL QUALIFYING

Notts (Hollinwell) 2 July
Andrew Wilson, England
Thomas Thurloway [a]**, England**
Ashton Turner [p]**, England**

Prince's 2 July
Curtis Knipes [a]**, England**
Callum Shinkwin, England
Austin Connelly, Canada

St Annes Old Links 2 July
Garrick Porteous, England
Jack Senior, England
Matthew Baldwin, England

Fairmont St Andrews 2 July
Brandon Wu [a]**, USA**
Connor Syme, Scotland
Sam Locke, Scotland

[a] Denotes amateur   [p] Qualified after play-off

KOREA

KOLON Korea Open 20-23 June
Innchoon Hwang, Korea
Dongkyu Jang, Korea

JAPAN

The Mizuno Open 30 May - 2 June
Yuta Ikeda, Japan
Chan Kim, USA
Sang Hyun Park, Korea
Gunn Charoenkul, Thailand

SINGAPORE

SMBC Singapore Open 17-20 January
Jazz Janewattananond, Thailand
Yoshinori Fujimoto, Japan
Prom Meesawat, Thailand
Doyeob Mun, Korea

AUSTRALIA

Emirates Australian Open 15-18 November 2018
Abraham Ancer, Mexico
Dimitrios Papadatos, Australia
Jake McLeod, Australia

Rory McIlroy

Danny Willett

Tommy Fleetwood

Name, Country	Category
Byeong Hun An, Korea	4
Kiradech Aphibarnrat, Thailand	4,5
Yosuke Asaji, Japan	20
Isidro Benitez, Mexico	14
Lucas Bjerregaard, Denmark	4,5
Alexander Björk, Sweden	5
Keegan Bradley, USA	4,12
Rafa Cabrera Bello, Spain	4,5
Jorge Campillo, Spain	5
Patrick Cantlay, USA	4,12
Paul Casey, England	4,12,15
Stewart Cink, USA	1,2
Darren Clarke, Northern Ireland	1,2
Corey Conners, Canada	4
Joel Dahmen, USA	4
Jason Day, Australia	4,10,12
Bryson DeChambeau, USA	4,12,15
David Duval, USA	1
Ernie Els, South Africa	1,2
Tony Finau, USA	3,4,12,15
Matthew Fitzpatrick, England	4,5
Tommy Fleetwood, England	4,5,12,15
Rickie Fowler, USA	4,12,15
Ryan Fox, New Zealand	5
Jim Furyk, USA	4
Sergio Garcia, Spain	4,5,9,15
Lucas Glover, USA	4
Branden Grace, South Africa	4
Emiliano Grillo, Argentina	4
Justin Harding, South Africa	4
Brian Harman, USA	4
Padraig Harrington, Rep of Ireland	1
Tyrrell Hatton, England	4,5,15
Charley Hoffman, USA	4
JB Holmes, USA	4
Mikumu Horikawa, Japan	22
Billy Horschel, USA	4,12
Shugo Imahira, Japan	21
Yuki Inamori, Japan	19
Miguel Ángel Jiménez, Spain	23
Dustin Johnson, USA	4,8,12,15
Zach Johnson, USA	1,2
Takumi Kanaya [a], Japan	28
Si Woo Kim, Korea	11
Kevin Kisner, USA	3,4
Kurt Kitayama, USA	7
Patton Kizzire, USA	12
Russell Knox, Scotland	5
Brooks Koepka, USA	4,8,10,12,15
Jason Kokrak, USA	4
Mikko Korhonen, Finland	4
Matt Kuchar, USA	3,4
Paul Lawrie, Scotland	1
Tom Lehman, USA	1
Marc Leishman, Australia	4,12
Alex Levy, France	5
Tom Lewis, England	4
David Lipsky, USA	
Luke List, USA	
Zander Lombard, South Africa	18
Shane Lowry, Rep of Ireland	
Joost Luiten, Netherlands	
Robert MacIntyre, Scotland	
Hideki Matsuyama, Japan	4,12
Rory McIlroy, Northern Ireland	1,2,3,4,5,10,11,12,15
Jake McLeod, Australia	17
Phil Mickelson, USA	1,2,4,12,15
Francesco Molinari, Italy	1,2,3,4,5,6,12,15
Joaquin Niemann, Chile	
Alex Noren, Sweden	4,5,6,15
Shaun Norris, South Africa	2
Thorbjørn Olesen, Denmark	5,15
Louis Oosthuizen, South Africa	1,2,4
Adrian Otaegui, Spain	
Ryan Palmer, USA	12
CT Pan, Chinese Taipei	
Andrea Pavan, Italy	
Eddie Pepperell, England	3,4,5
Thomas Pieters, Belgium	
Ian Poulter, England	4,15
Andrew Putnam, USA	
Jon Rahm, Spain	4,5,12,15
Chez Reavie, USA	12
Patrick Reed, USA	4,5,9,12,15
Justin Rose, England	3,4,5,12,15
Rory Sabbatini, Slovakia	
Xander Schauffele, USA	3,4,5,12
Matthias Schmid [a], Germany	20
Adam Scott, Australia	
Shubhankar Sharma, India	5,16
Webb Simpson, USA	4,11,12,15
Cameron Smith, Australia	4,12
Brandt Snedeker, USA	
Jordan Spieth, USA	1,2,3,4,8,9,15
Kyle Stanley, USA	12
Henrik Stenson, Sweden	1,2,4,15
Richard Sterne, South Africa	
Brandon Stone, South Africa	5
Kevin Streelman, USA	
James Sugrue [a], Rep of Ireland	24
Andy Sullivan, England	5
Justin Thomas, USA	4,10,12,15
Erik van Rooyen, South Africa	
Jimmy Walker, USA	10
Matthew Wallace, England	4,5
Bubba Watson, USA	4,12,15
Lee Westwood, England	5
Danny Willett, England	5,9
Aaron Wise, USA	12
Chris Wood, England	6
Gary Woodland, USA	4,8,12
Tiger Woods, USA	1,3,4,9,12,15

Francesco Molinari, the 2018 Champion Golfer, returns the Claret Jug to Martin Slumbers, Chief Executive of The R&A.

KEY TO EXEMPTIONS FOR THE 148TH OPEN

Exemptions for 2019 were granted to the following:

(1) The Open Champions aged 60 or under on 21 July 2019.

(2) The Open Champions for 2009-2018.

(3) First 10 and anyone tying for 10th place in The 147th Open Championship (2018) at Carnoustie.

(4) The first 50 players on the Official World Golf Ranking for Week 21, 2019, with additional players and reserves drawn from the highest ranked non-exempt players in the weeks prior to The Open.

(5) First 30 in the Race to Dubai Rankings for 2018.

(6) The BMW PGA Championship winners for 2016-2018.

(7) First 5 European Tour members and any European Tour members tying for 5th place, not otherwise exempt, in the top 20 of the Race to Dubai Rankings on completion of the 2019 BMW International Open.

(8) The US Open Champions for 2015-2019.

(9) The Masters Tournament Champions for 2015-2019.

(10) The PGA Champions for 2014-2019.

(11) THE PLAYERS Champions for 2017-2019.

(12) The top 30 players from the 2018 FedExCup Points List.

(13) First 5 PGA TOUR members and any PGA TOUR members tying for 5th place, not exempt in the top 20 of the PGA TOUR FedExCup Points List for 2019 on completion of the 2019 Travelers Championship.

(14) The 113th VISA Open de Argentina 2018 Champion.

(15) Playing members of the 2018 Ryder Cup Teams.

(16) First and anyone tying for 1st place on the Order of Merit of the Asian Tour for 2018.

(17) First and anyone tying for 1st place on the Order of Merit of the PGA Tour of Australasia for 2018.

(18) First and anyone tying for 1st place on the Order of Merit of the Sunshine Tour for 2018.

(19) The Japan Open Champion for 2018.

(20) The Asia-Pacific Diamond Cup Champion for 2019.

(21) First 2 and anyone tying for 2nd place on the Official Money List of the Japan Golf Tour for 2018.

(22) First and anyone tying for 1st place, not exempt, in a cumulative money list taken from all official 2019 Japan Golf Tour events up to and including the 2019 Japan Tour Championship.

(23) The Senior Open Champion for 2018.

(24) The Amateur Champion for 2019.

(25) The US Amateur Champion for 2018.

(26) The European Amateur Champion for 2019.

(27) The Mark H McCormack Medal (Men's World Amateur Golf Ranking™) winner for 2018.

Riveting Return to Portrush

By Andy Farrell

Was there ever a more extraordinary comeback in golf than The Open's return to Royal Portrush?

It was a week the like of which few had ever experienced, let alone the Championship in its 148th staging. The first ever sold-out Open. The second highest attendance ever. A dramatic course almost universally praised by the players. And a home winner cheered to victory at full volume by the most passionate fans whatever the weather.

It was utterly riveting and now Max Faulkner, the 1951 Champion Golfer, has a fellow Portrush winner in Shane Lowry. But even Lowry's phenomenal performance cannot match the story of how The Open returned to Northern Ireland.

Carnoustie returned to The Open rota after 24 years and Royal Liverpool after 39. It was 68 years for Royal Portrush but forget getting the best players in the world to play in The Open; after the political turmoil and violence of the Troubles, which flared in the late 1960s, the first step was getting any golfers to return.

A new dawn for The Open at Royal Portrush.

When Wilma Erskine took over as Secretary-Manager of the club 35 years ago there were few overseas visitors. "We would go out and hug them we were so pleased they came," Erskine said.

Gradually, a new generation of golfers began once more enjoying the spectacular scenery — the Whiterocks cliffs, the Skerries out to sea and Islay of the Hebrides across the water, all just along the coast from Dunluce Castle and the Giant's Causeway — as well as fine links featuring many teasing doglegs and tricky humps and hollows around the greens, although the fewest bunkers of any Open course.

Even before the Good Friday Agreement of 1998, events also returned — The Amateur Championship in 1993 for the first time in 33 years and, two years later, the first of six Senior Opens. Fittingly, the first two were won by Brian Barnes, the son-in-law of Faulkner.

A decade later and Padraig Harrington, at Carnoustie in 2007, won the first of his two Opens. It came 60 years after Ireland's only other major champion, Fred Daly, who learnt the game as a caddie at Portrush, had lifted the Claret Jug. On the heels of Harrington came a trio of major

A replica of the Claret Jug in the Royal Portrush clubhouse with the medals won by Fred Daly and Darren Clarke.

champions from north of the border. Within 13 months, Portrush-born Graeme McDowell won the 2010 US Open; Rory McIlroy, the Portrush course record holder thanks to a 61 at the age of 16, won the 2011 US Open; and Portrush resident Darren Clarke won the 2011 Open.

The morning after Clarke's victory, Peter Dawson, then the Chief Executive of The R&A, was asked about Portrush's chances of staging The Open again. "We're all very well aware that three winners from Northern Ireland increases the interest level in this," he said. Not least, Dawson had heard about it from the new Champion Golfer of the Year at a reception the previous evening.

Before heading home to place his winner's medal alongside Daly's in the Royal Portrush clubhouse, Clarke admitted the logistical challenge facing The R&A would be huge but stated: "I would love to see it going to Royal Portrush because it is every bit as good as any Open venue on the rota right now."

Dawson was cautious. To stage The Open, they needed "a great course, plenty of infrastructure combined with the prospect of commercial success. No doubt about the golf course at Portrush, although there might be one or two things one would do, but the other two are what we need to look at. I don't want to start a hare running on this," he summarised, "other than we are going to take a look."

McDowell said: "It started as a joke, 'Why can't we go back?' Then the jokes turned serious." In 2012, the European Tour took the Irish Open back to Portrush for the first time since 1947. Jamie Donaldson was the winner and a Tour record 130,000 spectators turned up.

While it became apparent that a return to Northern Ireland could be a commercial success, McIlroy kept winning majors — four in all by 2014. "It became something of a tsunami," Dawson reflected. "The continued success of the Irish golfers, the changes to the golf course that were vital and when the Northern Ireland government came on board, it all had a momentum of its own."

Revamping the Dunluce Links created room around the new 18th for the modern grandstands and tented villages.

Darren Clarke with the participants in The R&A's 9 Hole Challenge won by the Royal Portrush pairing.

It took a collaborative effort to overcome the logistical hurdles, involving Royal Portrush Golf Club, led by Erskine, The R&A, the Northern Ireland government and local police service. "It's been a complete team effort and that's what I am most proud of," said Johnnie Cole-Hamilton, The R&A's Executive Director of Championships. With the club stepping up to stage The Amateur Championship in 2014, Dawson was able to announce the return of The Open prior to his retirement from The R&A. "I had a part in bringing it here," he said at The 148th Open, "but the way the

R&A takes the initiative on water bottles

Five decades ago David Attenborough helped transform coverage of The Open when, as an executive at the BBC, he oversaw the introduction of colour television. Now the world famous naturalist has again inspired a profound change at The 148th Open with the removal from Royal Portrush of single-use plastic water bottles.

Instead, drinking water refilling stations were installed across Royal Portrush for fans to use with their own refillable bottles or The Open's own stainless steel bottles. Over 5,000 of the bottles, provided by Bluewater, were given away free to fans, staff and media, while the competitors received their own special Players' Edition. The Open Water initiative was part of the ongoing GreenLinks sustainability programme, which saw the elimination of plastic straws in 2018, and was supported by the UN Environment's Clean Seas campaign, which raises awareness of global marine plastic pollution.

"Like lots of people we took notice of David Attenborough's *Blue Planet* documentary and the call to arms to do more on marine plastic pollution," said Johnnie Cole-Hamilton, Executive Director of Championships. "To remove single-use plastic water bottles from the site is something we are very proud of and we're very pleased we've had huge cooperation from lots of our partners on that."

"For a number of years we have looked at recycling, reducing waste to landfill to close to zero," added Martin Slumbers, Chief Executive of The R&A. "This year was a step forward on single-use plastic water bottles and we will look to do more on plastics in the coming year. The whole game needs to look at sustainability and water conservation. We have started a project called Golf Course 2030 to look at how to maintain the playing surfaces we have today with a fraction of the water usage and no pesticides, no fertilisers. It will create great opportunities for the game."

Tyrrell Hatton and (above) Tommy Fleetwood with their own Players' Edition water bottle.

A new tunnel in the dunes allowed players access between certain greens and tees without spoiling the view for fans.

Championship has been presented is outstanding and that is down to many other people."

While a new train station and improved road access were among significant changes to the town, the course itself had to be revamped to accommodate the huge grandstands and tented villages of a modern Open. An innovative solution was found with the help of course designer Martin Ebert, who immersed himself in the history of the club to understand the evolution of the links.

A nine-hole course was first laid out in 1888, expanded to 18 holes the following year, playing away from the old clubhouse in town. The present course is based on Harry Colt's design from the 1930s. Colt's masterstroke was to stretch the course further on to the dramatic sand dunes to the east, reaching as far as the present fifth hole, which sweeps down to an infinity green perched 40 feet above the beach.

However, within a few years the land closest to the clubhouse, known as the "Triangle", was lost to the expansion of the town. PG Stevenson, the club professional, devised a plan to add two new holes, what are today the 10th and 11th holes, which opened in 1939. Colt approved of the plan, wondering why he had not thought to use the land himself. Bernard Darwin certainly approved when he saw the modern Dunluce Links for the first time at the 1951 Open. "It is truly magnificent," he wrote in *The Times*. "Colt has built himself a monument more enduring than brass."

By then the original clubhouse had been abandoned and a new one established on its present site, east of the town. Ebert, taking inspiration from Colt and Stevenson, suggested moving the course further out onto the dunes by creating two new holes using land from the neighbouring Valley course. Then the old 17th and 18th holes, being relatively flat and out of character with the rest of the course, could be used for the tented

A jewel in the dunes — the new seventh hole, a par five with the "Big Nellie" bunker on the right in the foreground.

village and sundry other amenities. "We thought that was drastic," recalled Erskine, "but lo and behold, we communicated it to the members and they were on board." When put to the vote, the motion passed with a unanimous show of hands.

Ebert's new holes — the spectacular seventh, a par five featuring a replica of the "Big Nellie" bunker from the old 17th, and the eighth, a strong dogleg par four — opened in 2017 and appeared to blend in immediately. "It has definitely enhanced the course," said Clarke. "He's kept them in the style of Harry Colt and they have much more character than the holes they replaced."

A knock-on effect was that the old 14th, the par three known as Calamity Corner with a 230-yard carry over a chasm in the dunes, now as the 16th comes at a crucial time in the round. It is followed by a downhill par four that is potentially drivable and the sharp dog-leg-right 18th with out of bounds on the left. It was here, as the old 16th, that Faulkner played a stunning recovery shot during the third round in 1951. With his ball close to a barbed-wire fence, he swung with his four-wood in such a way to avoid shredding his hands that the ball flew well out of bounds before curving back to land on the green. "That's the finest shot I've ever seen," said his playing partner Frank Stranahan, the great American amateur.

Faulkner, a champion services boxer

Calamity Corner, the well-named 16th hole, is played over a chasm down to the Valley course below.

in World War II when he was a physical training instructor in the RAF, was a colourful character. With a big lead prior to the final round, the tale is told of Faulkner being asked for an autograph by a boy and adding: "1951 Open champion". Alas, it may have been fake news, invented by his Fleet Street ghostwriter. Lowry, certainly, did not dare to tempt fate in such a manner.

Any Portrush roll of honour must include Joe Carr, the legendary Irish amateur who won his third Amateur Championship there in 1960, while France's Catherine Lacoste claimed the Women's Amateur in 1969, two years after winning the US Women's Open. Joyce Wethered won the second of four Women's Amateur titles in 1924, following in the footsteps of Lady Margaret Scott, who won her third successive title at Portrush in 1895. Women's golf flourished in the early days of the club, with Rhona Adair winning two Women's Amateur titles and May Hezlet three. Two other Hezlet sisters, Florence and Violet, each finished as runners-up, while a brother, Charles, played in the Walker Cup.

That 1895 Women's Amateur Championship was only the third ever staged but was remembered as the most enjoyable of all by player-turned-administrator-turned-journalist Mabel Stringer. "The members of the club," she wrote, "left nothing undone which might contribute to the success, or pleasure, of the meeting."

Words that proved as true today as they were back then.

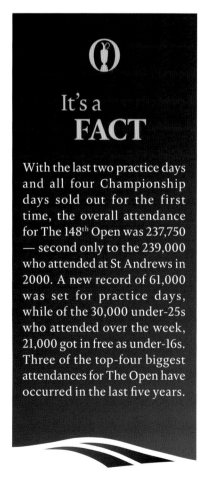

It's a
FACT

With the last two practice days and all four Championship days sold out for the first time, the overall attendance for The 148th Open was 237,750 — second only to the 239,000 who attended at St Andrews in 2000. A new record of 61,000 was set for practice days, while of the 30,000 under-25s who attended over the week, 21,000 got in free as under-16s. Three of the top-four biggest attendances for The Open have occurred in the last five years.

Irish golf making its own luck

Lewine Mair on how The Open made such a successful return to Portrush

That everything came together so well at Royal Portrush was down to townsfolk understanding golf and golfers perhaps as well as anywhere in the world. From Wilma Erskine, the Secretary-Manager of Royal Portrush, to those sweeping the streets, they operated as a team, with each individual as overjoyed as the next at the successful return of The Open.

The saying, "The luck of the Irish", had its origins in a troubled past, moments in history when the Irish were distinctly unlucky. "Because of the past," said Tom Turner, who was in charge of the buggies ferrying the players to and from the practice ground, "we've tended not to have too high expectations. Now, when something goes right, like when we win at golf, or host an event such as this, we celebrate."

Alison Kearney, another of the volunteers and one whose smile was not to be washed away by any amount of rain, was of the opinion that the Irish, post Troubles, were all the happier for concentrating on simple things, with family life leading the way. "We're definitely a happy lot," she said, "and, yes, we think we're lucky."

At the same time, she thought that the Troubles had contributed to golf's astonishing growth. "When they were at their most intense, parents would see the local club as 'a safe place' for their children. Golf crossed the divide. All the kids played, and what we have today is a situation in which everyone who lives within five miles of a golf club knows everything there is to know about the game."

You knew that Shane Lowry, with the shamrocks on his golf balls, would be a believer in Irish luck. When asked to confirm as much at the start of the week, he gave an enthusiastic nod before describing himself as someone who was serious about his golf whilst having more of a "happy-go-lucky" attitude than most. "To use another old saying," he added, "I'd say that my glass is half full as opposed to half empty." (It might have been rather more than that come the Sunday.)

Callaway went to town on a Lucky Irish theme, providing golf bags (right) for all their players, with the backcloth to the emerald exterior a mass of hexagons by way of a tribute to the nearby Giant's Causeway and its interlocking basalt columns. These, as the story goes, served as a set of steps for an Irish giant who arranged to do battle with his Scottish equivalent.

No one would pretend that Rory McIlroy was lucky as he had an opening eight and a closing seven in

Portrush's Championship links is named after Dunluce Castle.

McIlroy was one of those children for whom golf had served as a shield from the Troubles, Graeme McDowell another. Again, Royal Portrush was a perfect example of a club which took juniors under its wing. In which connection, Ross Hallett, an executive of IMG, told how he had been visiting Portrush on a regular basis since 1997 and that nothing had struck him more across the years than the way in which the club had embraced its juniors. "On any Friday/Saturday night in the summer, the putting green was always busy with a few or many kids hanging about with their putters, having fun, and improving all the while."

Wilma Erskine, it has to be said, trained her charges well. Indeed, when she and McDowell were being

his first-round 79. The crowds around the first tee and the weight of expectation got to him. Yet there was another side to his week; one which left people glowing at the memory of how their favourite son dealt with his disappointment in missing the cut by a single shot.

To no small degree, he eschewed the "Poor me" approach to praise the fans who had stayed to the

bitter end of his losing battle; and to say how they had played their part in making the Championship a grand success story even if he himself had fallen short. One commentator after another assured him that his classy acceptance of defeat had ensured that that was not the case.

honoured at the 2019 Association of Golf Writers' dinner (above, with Francesco Molinari), McDowell made humorous mention of the week he had carried a mobile scoreboard at one of the club's post-Troubles tournaments. Wilma had been the custodian of the pay-packets and, according to McDowell, it had taken all the guts in the golfing world to hammer at the office door of someone so powerful.

Looking back on The 148th Open, the Championship didn't just have one winner in the redoubtable Shane Lowry. All the Irish felt like winners and the process of celebrating their lucky lot could have as long a run as *The Mousetrap*, which, amazingly enough, opened the year after Royal Portrush last hosted The Open.

JB at Home on Field of Drama

By Andy Farrell

This was golf's *Field of Dreams* moment. If you build it they will come.

They came all right. The Dunluce Links at Royal Portrush had to be rebuilt — along with parts of the town — to accommodate The 148th Open but the reward was a sold-out attendance for the first time in the Championship's long history.

They came to this field of drama and found dreams and nightmares unfolding in front of them in almost equal measure. Anticipation and excitement, the like of which had rarely been seen before as The Open returned to Northern Ireland for the first time in 68 years, was met with golf as wildly unpredictable as the weather on the Antrim coast.

Good and bad, delight and disaster, the twists kept coming. For Shane Lowry being cheered on by the home fans, there was Rory McIlroy in need of consolation and being cheered up. For JB Holmes leading the way on five-under-par, there was fellow American Phil Mickelson trailing at five-over-par. For Brooks Koepka's inevitable and intimidating presence on the leaderboard, there was Tiger Woods' absence from it.

For Darren Clarke's birdie at the first, there was Graeme McDowell's triple-bogey at the last. For Tommy Fleetwood's consistency, there was Francesco Molinari being atypically erratic. For Emiliano Grillo's hole-in-one at the 13th, there was David Duval's 14 at the seventh. This was sport in the raw.

Early morning sunshine graced the opening tee shot, an honour bestowed on Clarke, the 2011 Champion Golfer. A birdie delivered with a 15-foot putt followed and he turned to give a wave down the hill to the thousands of dawn-risers lining the fairway.

It got better. Clarke almost holed his tee shot at the short third and then got up and down for a birdie at the fifth to go to three-under-par. James Sugrue, the 22-year-old from County Cork who the month previously won The Amateur Championship at Portmarnock, a good Irish omen perhaps, was playing alongside Clarke and admitted to being as nervous as he ever has. But birdies at the second and sixth holes settled him down.

With his lowest score in The Open, JB Holmes took the lead.

Darren Clarke had the honour of hitting the first tee shot.

The rain arrived and Clarke appeared to be playing through a rainbow on the new seventh. A six was his first dropped shot of a day that saw him finish up with a level-par 71 after two late bogeys. Sugrue also had a 71, although the youngster would have been one better but for his eagle putt at the 12th, set up by a superb three-wood into the green, not sitting on the lip.

Lowry was soon taking up the baton. He birdied the third and almost holed his tee shot at the fifth, two-putting for a birdie-three. Then he birdied the ninth and 10th holes. He gave one back at the 11th but, at the 12th, recovered from thick rough with a good pitch to 12 feet and holed for the birdie. Six pars followed as the 32-year-old from Clara took the clubhouse lead on 67. "I missed a few chances coming in but I think four-under is a great score on that course," Lowry said.

He hit 16 greens in regulation, more than anyone else all day, but when he did get out of position, he

When the rain arrived, Clarke appeared to be playing through a rainbow on the long seventh hole.

Fans line the first hole at Royal Portrush on a day The Open sold out in advance for the first time ever.

Ireland's Shane Lowry led for much of the first day, accompanied by his caddie Brian "Bo" Martin.

Clarke with Amateur champion James Sugrue.

wrong side of the hole, you can get yourself into a whole lot of trouble. But if you play all right you can make some birdies as well and thankfully I did that today."

As for the support he received, the big man, who first came to prominence by winning the Irish Open as an amateur in 2009, was already showing signs of revelling in the atmosphere. "I thoroughly enjoyed today. The crowds were unbelievable. Being cheered on every tee box and every green is such a special feeling. I tried to enjoy it as much as I could while I was doing my work and getting down to business.

"It's going to be an exciting few days ahead," he added. "I hope I can give them something to cheer about on Sunday afternoon."

Lowry's once hero, now friend Padraig Harrington carded a 75 but Portrush's own McDowell was making steady progress with his third birdie of

again showed his famous recovery skills. "Where my game's at now, if I hit a bad shot, I feel I can get myself out of trouble," he said. "This golf course is tricky in parts. If you miss it on the

Late night thrill for Turner

Out in the last game of the day, Ashton Turner had the thrill of seeing his name on The Open leaderboards. The 23-year-old qualifier from Lincolnshire, who won a play-off at the third extra hole for the last spot at Notts (Hollinwell), was just two behind until a bogey at the last gave him a 69 finishing just before 9.30pm. "I played really well and it was hard to avoid all the leaderboards out on the course," Turner said.

"There was not much time to enjoy it, a case of get back, have something to eat and get some sleep. I did not play quite as well the next couple of days but to make the cut was great and a big improvement on last year." Out first on Sunday morning, the EuroPro Tour player finished with his best score of the week, a 68.

Turner made his debut in The Open at Carnoustie in 2018 when he caught the attention of the media due to his unusual backstory. He suffered from childhood cerebral palsy, discovered after he fell in a fish tank and cracked his skull as a one-year-old. For the first six years of his life he struggled to walk due to coordination and balance issues. Golf was suggested as a sport to complement the intensive physiotherapy that he had to undergo. "I was expecting playing in The Open to be a big thing," Turner said. "Then it got even bigger when the story came out."

Two-time Champion Golfer Padraig Harrington was disappointed with an opening 75.

the day at the 14th. Then shots went with three-putts at the 15th and 17th holes before he lost a ball in the rough at the last and took a seven for a 73. "Such a special day," he said. "To play as well as I did and then finish like that, it hurts a lot. Listen, you have to take the rough with the smooth and that was rough. Hopefully, there is some more smooth ahead."

Not for McIlroy, alas. "Go Rory," proclaimed the banners — just not *there*. He had been out of bounds on the right of the first hole in his Wednesday practice round and now over-corrected and went too far left. Many a visitor has done exactly that before, and will again, but McIlroy was extending the ever warm Irish welcome too far in making them feel better about themselves.

A female spectator had the screen of her mobile phone cracked as the ball plunged into the crowd. Everyone with a heart felt the fissures open up with what happened next. McIlroy again pulled his next tee shot, albeit short of the boundary line.

Graeme McDowell started well but slipped to a 73.

Rory McIlroy reacts to going out of bounds at the first hole … where he also took a drop for an unplayable lie.

He drove into the rough at the fifth but salvaged a par.

A triple-bogey at the 18th hole meant a shocked McIlroy finished with an eight-over-par 79.

England's Tyrrell Hatton chips at the 15th hole on the way to a three-under-par 68.

His fourth, rather than seeking short grass, found more rough left of the green. It was a spot so thick that he had to take an unplayable for his fifth. A chip and two putts gave him an opening eight.

It got worse. He failed to birdie the second and went long at the third, dropping another shot. Birdies at the seventh and ninth holes salvaged an outward 39 and a string of pars followed. Hard to believe that a round of 79 could contain a stretch of 12 holes played in two-under-par with no dropped shots. His stout recovery work was undone with a double-bogey at the 16th, Calamity Corner indeed, which included a casually missed tap-in. "Inexcusable," he said.

McIlroy again found the rough at the last and took two hacks to get back to the fairway, then missed the green with his approach. A triple-bogey to finish, like McDowell. It was not McIlroy's worst score in The Open, that was an 80 in 2010 at St Andrews that followed an opening 63. In 2013 at Muirfield, he also opened with a 79, the only time he had missed the cut in his home major. Was there a way back to the cut line? he was asked. "Definitely a way back to Florida," he joked.

"I was nervous because it's an Open Championship," he said when asked if playing at home had become too much. "I usually get nervous on the first tee, regardless of where. Maybe a little

It's a FACT

Ryan Fox set a new record for the second nine of any course in The Open with 29 strokes. The old record of 30 was first achieved by Eric Brown at Royal Lytham & St Annes in 1958. Denis Durnian holds the record for the first nine holes of 28 strokes at Royal Birkdale in 1983.

EXCERPTS FROM THE PRESS

"Tiger Woods, Rory McIlroy and Phil Mickelson might be the three most popular golfers in the world. They're also all likely to be firing up their respective private jets tomorrow afternoon for an early trip back home."

—Daniel Rapaport,
Sports Illustrated

"The crowd was begging for an Irish story and where McIlroy failed, Lowry delivered in spades."

—Brian Keogh,
Irish Independent

"The Dunluce Links has a 16th hole called Calamity and a 17th called Purgatory, but McIlroy got a grim, bitter taste of both of those things at the very first hole..."

—Nick Rodger,
The Herald

"Links golf is typically played on rock-hard fairways filled with quirky bounces, blind shots that require aiming at a white-painted rock or taking a line over a church steeple or a smokestack in the distance."

—Adam Schupak,
Morning Read

A 68 for Sergio Garcia was the Spaniard's best round of the week.

A steady start for Lee Westwood on three-under-par.

Lowry got through Calamity Corner, the 236-yard 16th hole, with a par as he revelled in the atmosphere.

more today but I don't think it was that. I didn't give a very good account of myself. I can definitely play better. It was the simple stuff, getting the ball in the fairway, missing in the right spots if you do miss, taking advantage of the par fives — I only birdied one of those today — things I usually do pretty well I didn't do today and it made for a tough start."

Also off to a tough start was another fan favourite, Tiger Woods. The thrilling comeback victory at the Masters Tournament was but a memory. He had played only three times since winning at Augusta National and went on a family holiday in Thailand following the US Open. The cool, rainy, blustery conditions were not kind on his ailing back as the 43-year-old's gingerly movements made plain. A four at the first received a fist pump for "one of the best pars you've ever seen. It was kind of downhill from there. I am just not moving as well as I'd like and not able to shape the ball, everything was off the heel. Just Father Time."

It was a sad sight, as was that of Duval's travails at the seventh, which followed birdies at the first two holes and then an eight at the fifth. He lost his first two balls off the seventh tee, then

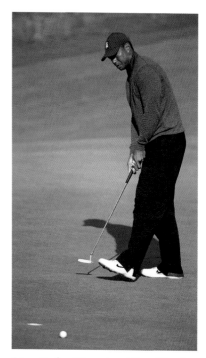

More Father Time than Tiger Woods, a day when the putts would not drop.

A game of two halves for Fox

When Ryan Fox began his Open campaign with a bogey at the first hole, he could have been forgiven for thinking it was not going to be his day. Yet by the time he was signing his card for a round of 68, the New Zealander was reflecting on the fact that he had become the first player in the long and storied history of the Championship to record a score of 29 on the inward nine.

After an outward half of 39, which included further dropped shots at the third and ninth holes, there was little hint of the fireworks that were to come. Fox — the son of Grant, the former All Blacks rugby union international — claimed his first birdie of the day at the 12th and then added five more for good measure, his only par coming with a three at the 16th hole.

Playing in his fourth Open, Fox had missed the halfway cut in his previous seven events and was as surprised as anyone suddenly to find himself in the record books. "That's pretty cool," he said when told of his achievement. "I did actually ask my caddie, 'Has anyone shot 29 for nine holes in a major?' And he said, 'Shut up and just hole the putts.' It's the first time I've had fun on a golf course for a while and you don't expect to do that."

The lowest nine ever in The Open was by Englishman Denis Durnian, who covered the front nine in 28 at Royal Birkdale in 1983.

Three birdies for American Tony Finau in his 68.

Brooks Koepka's only bogey came at the 17th hole.

in trying to find the third ended up playing a wrong ball almost to the green. With a two-shot penalty, back he went once more to play eight off the tee. It eventually added up to a 14 and a 91 for the 2001 Champion Golfer, who maintained his dignity in signing his card, fronting up to the media, and teeing-up again the next day despite an arm injury.

Back at the top of the leaderboard, 2012 US Open champion Webb Simpson, a member of the winning American Walker Cup team at Royal County Down in 2007, got to five-under-par before bogeying the last two holes. Jon Rahm also got to the same mark later in the day before the two-time Irish Open winner, including at nearby Portstewart in 2017, missed a short par putt at the 15th. He also dropped a shot at the last.

Rahm and Simpson were among 13 players who finished on 68, including perennial Open contenders Sergio Garcia and Lee Westwood, who brightened up his day with birdies at the 16th and 18th holes. Fleetwood did not drop a shot in his

No dropped shots for Tommy Fleetwood in a 68.

Round of the Day: JB Holmes – 66

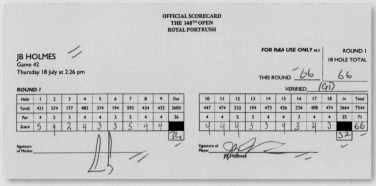

OFFICIAL SCORECARD
THE 148TH OPEN
ROYAL PORTRUSH

JB HOLMES
Game 42
Thursday 18 July at 2.26 pm

FOR R&A USE ONLY *413*

THIS ROUND `66`

ROUND 1
18 HOLE TOTAL

`66`

VERIFIED `(GT)`

ROUND 1

Hole	1	2	3	4	5	6	7	8	9	Out	10	11	12	13	14	15	16	17	18	In	Total
Yards	421	574	177	482	374	194	592	434	432	3680	447	474	532	194	473	426	236	408	474	3664	7344
Par	4	5	3	4	4	3	5	4	4	36	4	4	5	3	4	4	3	4	4	35	71
Score	5	4	2	4	3	3	5	4	4	34	4	4	4	3	3	4	3	4	3	32	66

Signature of Marker

Signature of Player
JB Holmes

Spain's Jon Rahm led briefly before two late bogeys.

68; Tony Finau and Kiradech Aphibarnrat could say the same. As for Fleetwood's "Moliwood" Ryder Cup partner, the defending Champion, who played his last 37 holes at Carnoustie without a bogey, managed only five holes at Portrush before dropping a shot at the sixth.

Molinari then took a double-bogey at the eighth on the way to an untidy 74. A year ago the Italian had arrived at The Open late from the John Deere Classic in America high in form and low in expectation. This year he had not played in three weeks and was low in form and high in expectation. No wonder his usually solid game developed a few uncharacteristic errors.

A nightmare 14 for David Duval at the seventh.

A 68 for Scottish left-hander Robert MacIntyre on debut.

Webb Simpson got to five-under-par before bogeys at the last two holes.

An inconsistent day for 2018 Champion Golfer Francesco Molinari.

"A day Royal Portrush will never forget; a day Rory McIlroy will never want to remember."

—James Corrigan,
The Daily Telegraph

"The arm-spreading gesture to the gallery after holing a long one for that solitary birdie summed up what Tiger thought of his day with the putter."

—Andy Dunn,
Daily Mirror

"We have said this before about McIlroy. He wins big and he loses big. This was epic by any measure. It could have been worse."

—Kevin Garside,
i newspaper

"Shane Lowry, one of golf's good guys, would be a hugely popular winner here."

—Martin Dempster,
The Scotsman

"Never mind swinging a golf club, there was barely enough room to swing a cat at Royal Portrush yesterday as the town that dared to dream the impossible dream welcomed the world to the biggest sporting event in Northern Ireland's history with open arms."

—Ivan Little,
Belfast Telegraph

Leader Holmes, who once played at the Dunluce Links when he was in college, drives at the 17th hole.

Dylan Frittelli, the last man to secure his place at Portrush by winning this year's John Deere Classic the previous Sunday night, was one of a group on 68 who bogeyed the last, that also included young Scottish left-hander Robert MacIntyre and England's Tyrrell Hatton. Then there was Ryan Fox, who went 39-29 to set a new second-nine record for The Open and, ominously, Koepka. The American, who had not finished outside the top two in the last four majors, was four-under-par after 14 holes and looking to build another solid challenge. He was helped greatly by having a caddie in Ricky Elliott who learned to play at Portrush. "I don't have to learn much, my caddie knows it all," Koepka said. Other than a bogey at the 17th, he was in good shape.

But, as it turned out, two behind the leader at the end of the day. Holmes, out late in the afternoon, bogeyed the first hole before birdieing three of the next four. There the man from Kentucky quietly sat, just off the top of the leaderboard, until he got up and down for a four at the 12th, holed a 20-footer for a three at the 14th and hit a cut five-iron to 15 feet at the last to take the lead on 66. This was his lowest score in The Open by two strokes.

Although Holmes had won the Genesis Open in February, his form of late was patchy. He withdrew after one round of the Wells Fargo Championship and then missed his next five cuts before a steadying 21st place at the Rocket Mortgage Classic in Detroit. "My results didn't show it but I felt confident coming in here," said the 37-year-old American. "Something clicked in Detroit and I've been hitting it great. I didn't miss too many shots and just stuck to the game plan of not getting too greedy going for pins. Try to hit the fat of the green and hopefully make some putts."

Any sort of local knowledge was thought to be key, given that everyone was playing in The Open on the Dunluce Links for the first time, and this was not Holmes' first visit to Portrush. A college trip to Ireland had provided his first taste of links golf though it was sufficiently long ago for the memory to be hazy. "We played one round here and I don't remember all the holes," he said. "Unfortunately, the caddies we had weren't used to somebody hitting 320 yards so I got some bad lines."

By Thursday night, when the local caddies gathered at the Harbour Bar in town, no doubt the tale was that they had taught The Open leader all he knew.

FIRST ROUND LEADERS

HOLE	1	2	3	4	5	6	7	8	9	10	11	12	13	14	15	16	17	18	TOTAL
PAR	4	5	3	4	4	3	5	4	4	4	4	5	3	4	4	3	4	4	
JB Holmes	5	4	2	4	3	3	5	4	4	4	4	4	3	3	4	3	4	3	66
Shane Lowry	4	5	2	4	3	5	4	3	3	5	4	3	4	4	4	3	4	4	67
Alex Noren	3	5	3	3	4	3	5	3	5	4	3	4	3	5	4	3	4	4	68
Webb Simpson	4	5	4	4	3	4	3	4	3	3	5	2	4	4	3	4	5	5	68
Sergio Garcia	4	5	3	4	4	3	4	3	5	4	3	4	4	3	4	4	3	4	68
Dylan Frittelli	4	5	3	4	4	3	5	3	4	3	4	3	4	3	4	3	3	4	68
Robert MacIntyre	3	4	3	5	2	3	4	4	5	4	4	4	3	5	4	3	3	5	68
K Aphibarnrat	4	4	4	3	4	3	5	4	4	3	5	4	3	4	4	3	4	4	68
Ryan Fox	5	5	4	4	4	3	5	4	5	4	4	2	3	3	3	3	3	3	68
Tyrrell Hatton	4	5	3	4	3	3	5	4	4	4	4	3	3	4	4	3	4	4	68
Tommy Fleetwood	4	5	2	4	4	3	4	4	5	2	4	4	4	3	4	4	4	4	68
Brooks Koepka	4	4	3	4	3	3	5	4	4	4	4	3	3	4	3	4	5	4	68
Lee Westwood	4	5	3	5	3	2	4	4	4	4	5	4	3	5	4	2	4	3	68
Tony Finau	4	5	3	3	4	3	5	4	4	3	4	4	4	4	4	3	4	4	68
Jon Rahm	4	4	3	3	4	3	4	3	3	4	5	4	3	4	5	3	4	5	68

■ EAGLE OR BETTER   ■ BIRDIES   □ PAR   ■ OVER PAR

SCORING SUMMARY

FIRST ROUND SCORES

Players Under Par	41
Players At Par	12
Players Over Par	103

LOW SCORES

Low First Nine Jon Rahm	31
Low Second Nine Ryan Fox	29
Low Round JB Holmes	66

FIRST ROUND HOLE SUMMARY

HOLE	PAR	YARDS	EAGLES	BIRDIES	PARS	BOGEYS	D.BOGEYS	OTHER	RANK	AVERAGE
1	4	424	0	13	109	26	6	2	8	4.205
2	5	576	3	62	83	6	2	0	18	4.628
3	3	175	0	21	111	24	0	0	13	3.019
4	4	480	0	11	108	28	8	1	6	4.237
5	4	368	2	35	103	12	1	3	16	3.904
6	3	185	0	8	107	37	3	1	4	3.244
7	5	586	0	27	91	37	0	1	11	5.122
8	4	423	0	21	107	26	2	0	12	4.058
9	4	427	0	16	96	38	5	1	7	4.224
OUT	**36**	**3,644**	**5**	**214**	**915**	**234**	**27**	**9**		**36.641**
10	4	440	0	28	107	18	3	0	14	3.974
11	4	452	0	14	77	55	9	1	1	4.404
12	5	529	0	58	78	17	3	0	17	4.776
13	3	200	1	22	118	13	2	0	15	2.955
14	4	458	0	17	99	38	2	0	10	4.160
15	4	424	0	17	88	45	5	1	3	4.263
16	3	222	0	7	105	43	1	0	4	3.244
17	4	398	0	16	104	27	7	2	9	4.199
18	4	462	0	13	82	53	6	2	2	4.372
IN	**35**	**3,585**	**1**	**192**	**858**	**309**	**38**	**6**		**36.346**
TOTAL	**71**	**7,229**	**6**	**406**	**1,773**	**543**	**65**	**15**		**72.987**

For an Open it was actually pretty good. It rained off and on, the wind kicked up at times, but I've played before where it was miserable.
—JB Holmes

I felt very unconfident on the first tee, I'm not going to lie.
—Shane Lowry

It's beautiful, one of the most beautiful courses I've ever seen.
—Alex Noren

I teed-off one year at the Masters behind Jack, Gary and Arnold but I think this one with Darren Clarke topped it. I was happy to be part of it.
—Charley Hoffman

The crowd's been great. Just amazing. It's always surreal.
—Andrew "Beef" Johnston

Meeting 'Beef' for the first time was brilliant. The roar that erupted when 'Beef' stepped on the first tee made me chuckle a wee bit.
—Robert MacIntyre

Getting off that first tee this morning, I literally had a tear in my eye. It was kind of cool stuff.
—Graeme McDowell

Especially on the eighth, after a good tee shot in the middle of the fairway, with a wedge in my hands, I wasn't obviously expecting a double-bogey.
—Francesco Molinari

I feel like I played two rounds out there today.
—Jon Rahm

The Open returns — 'Wow!'

Philip Reid on an emotional roller coaster of a day at Royal Portrush

Darren Clarke celebrates a birdie on the opening hole.

In *Waiting for Godot*, by the Irish playwright Samuel Beckett, who as it happens loved his golf and was known for putting with a two-iron, the principals were left waiting in vain for the arrival of the man in the play's title. There was never any fear Darren Clarke would leave anyone waiting, as he answered the call for a 6.35am first strike of club face to ball.

From shortly after 6am, spectators had giddily gathered in the horse-shoe grandstand around the first tee. On cue, Clarke — his silver hair slicked back — arrived onto the tee, with the Amateur champion James Sugrue and the American green-gloved Charley Hoffman as witnesses to a piece of golfing history as the Portrush resident got The 148th Open under way, some 68 years after the Dunluce Links last staged the Championship.

Clarke's opening tee shot and then approach and a birdie putt provided the perfect start to the Championship, signalling as it did an emotional roller coaster of a day where his fellow Northern Irishmen Rory McIlroy and Graeme McDowell were cast as fall guys in the drama while Shane Lowry, who had sought to sneak in under the radar, was immediately cast into the spotlight with a superbly crafted first-round 67.

"Just everything about it, when I was about to hit my tee shot ... wow!" said Clarke of his emotions on the first tee, where he received a rapturous reception from the crowds with many capturing the moment on their smart phones.

But it would be the fate that befell McIlroy, some hours later, which left those in the grandstand and packed deep along the first fairway in a state of stunned silence. Using an iron off the tee, McIlroy pulled his opening shot so far to the left that it finished in the internal out-of-bounds, a triangle of land between the first and 18th holes that historically has been a no-go area for golf balls.

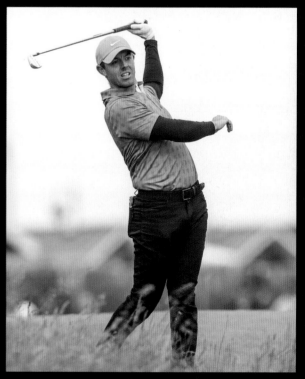

A round book-ended by disasters for Rory McIlroy.

Every vantage point was taken by the crowd, many giddy with excitement at the return of The Open to Portrush.

It wasn't just the crowd which was shell-shocked. So too was McIlroy, who grimaced and gritted his teeth as the ball flew ever leftwards. His second effort — playing three off the tee — was only marginally better, as it was again pulled left into heavy rough but short of the white stakes. And on it went, as the world number three struggled his way up to the hole, finding bracken alongside a greenside bunker and running up a horrendous quadruple-bogey-eight that effectively ended his Open challenge before it ever got going.

McIlroy's round of 79 was book-ended by disasters, a quadruple on the first and a triple on the 18th. But it was a double-bogey-five on the 16th, that giant of a par three known as Calamity Corner, which lingered most in his mind, for it was there he absent-mindedly went to tap in a short putt and missed the hole. "That was inexcusable. Tee shots like the first happen, you can get one riding on the wind a little too much. But lapses of concentration like that ... I sort of hit it on the run and missed it. And if I look back, it's probably the shot I'm disappointed about the most."

McIlroy wasn't alone in being hard done-by. McDowell (above), Portrush born and bred, and who had grown up learning his craft on the links

was undone by a lost ball in the rough on the 18th. In fact, his ball was discovered, but 12 seconds after the allotted three minutes search time had expired; a sour taste to finish his round, to be sure.

And while American JB Holmes carded a five-under-par 66 to claim the first-round lead, it was Lowry — who had been so nervous on the eve of the Championship that he had sneaked away to a quiet corner of the Bushmills Inn for a coffee and a chat with his coach Neil Manchip, to steady those nerves — who kept a steady course to manoeuvre his way into position.

"It's The Open, it's in Ireland. I'm playing well and I feel I should come up and do well. Why shouldn't I feel uneasy?" asked Lowry of that pre-Championship state of tension.

Yet, once on the links itself, and on a cantankerous old day on the Causeway Coast, one that didn't know right from wrong and which brought vagaries of heavy rain with flashes of sunshine, Lowry's 67 strokes meant that plan of flying in under the radar was well and truly thrown away in the wind.

On a roller coaster day of emotions for Messrs Clarke McIlroy and McDowell, the 32-year-old from Clara in County Offaly, in the heart of the island of Ireland had navigated a route towards a life-changing feat

McIlroy Does Not Go Gently

By Andy Farrell

"Do not go gentle into that good night," wrote Dylan Thomas. "Rage, rage against the dying of the light."

For a most dramatic enactment of those words, first published by the revered Welsh poet in 1951, the only year Royal Portrush had previously hosted The Open before its glorious return in 2019, you needed to witness a Northern Irishman try to keep alive his dream of winning the Claret Jug in front of his home fans on a cool, dank Friday evening.

To do so Rory McIlroy had to make the halfway cut in The 148th Open. And he had to do so after opening with a 79 in the first round. "Now, I wouldn't want to start from here," as visitors to the island seeking directions have often been told.

Yet Rory let his golf do the raging. He refused to go gently into the night and nor would his supporters let him. In scenes more reminiscent of a Sunday at The Open, no one dared leave despite the lateness of the hour. He needed them too much and he was producing sporting theatre of the highest

quality. By the time he got to the 18th hole there was not a seat to be had in the grandstands, not that anyone was sitting. A standing ovation was the least this performance deserved.

Earlier, Shane Lowry had joined JB Holmes in the lead, with Tommy Fleetwood and Lee Westwood just behind, but this was a mighty climax to another rousing day's golf at Portrush. It was already deep into the afternoon when McIlroy set out slightly sheepishly for his second round. As you would at eight-over-par when the lead was eight-under-par. But once Lowry had returned a second successive 67 to tie Holmes, somehow McIlroy sensed the spotlight had moved back onto him.

Its harsh glare had been too much on Thursday when he opened with an eight at the first. This time he parred the first two and then birdied the third from 25 feet. Another birdie at the seventh had him out in 34, still too far from safety.

In a similar situation, Tiger Woods had birdied the first and the sixth holes but it had not been the prelude to a miracle extension of his stay in Northern Ireland. It was a respectable round of 70, following a 78 the day before, with bogeys at

---

Late-night drama: Rory McIlroy pitches from the rough at the 17th hole in his quest to make the halfway cut.

Japan's Takumi Kanaya, the Asia-Pacific Amateur champion, narrowly misses a putt at the 18th to continue.

Tiger Woods salutes the fans after a 70.

the last two holes neither here nor there in terms of making the cut. "I just want to go home," said a weary 43-year-old.

A major season that had started on an incredible high at the Masters Tournament ended as only the second of his career in which he missed multiple cuts. And for the first time in the 83 majors they had both participated in, both Woods and Phil Mickelson, after a 76 and a 74, failed to qualify for the weekend.

At the other end of their careers, none of the amateurs in the field made the cut. James Sugrue and Takumi Kanaya, the Asia-Pacific Amateur champion from Japan, came the closest on two-over-par. Amateur champion Sugrue was on course to make it until a triple-bogey at the 14th, which ranked the hardest hole of the second round.

There was an even more cruel guillotine dropped on Darren Clarke, who arrived at the 18th on level-par. However, like McIlroy and Graeme McDowell the previous day, he was undone by a triple at the last. He took two to get out of a fairway bunker and then had three putts on the green, a crushing blow for the 50-year-old local hero and 2011 Champion Golfer of the Year.

Shane Lowry charged into the lead with six birdies in the first 10 holes.

JB Holmes tees off at the first hole on the way to a 68 and a tie for the 36-hole lead with Lowry.

Also missing out on three-over-par was two-time Champion Golfer Padraig Harrington and the US Open champion from Pebble Beach, Gary Woodland. McDowell, the solitary Northern Irishman left in the field, and defending Champion Golfer Francesco Molinari both squeezed through on what turned out to be the mark of one-over-par. There was a chance it could go to two-over, but the closer McIlroy got to the promised land, the more resistant the cut line appeared to shifting.

McIlroy's charge of the light brigade began with a birdie at the 10th from 10 feet, before he hit his approach at the 11th to two feet and then claimed a four at the 12th. A bogey at the short 13th might have killed off the whole enterprise but back he came at the next with a drive and a six-iron to 12 feet for another birdie. He got up and down from a bunker at the 15th, then gained some revenge at Calamity Corner. A five on Thursday was followed by a two when he struck a majestic tee shot to 10 feet and holed the putt. By this time, had his ball dared wander off line, the crowd would have sucked it into the hole.

Pars, however, were the best he could do at the

Francesco Molinari kept his title defence alive by making the cut with a 69.

Gary Woodland, the US Open champion from Pebble Beach, missed out.

Xander Schauffele improved by nine strokes on round one with a 65 that equalled the low score of the day.

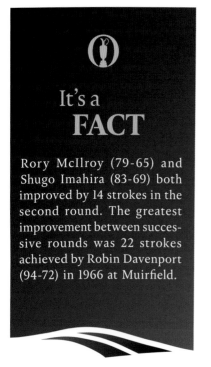

It's a
FACT

Rory McIlroy (79-65) and Shugo Imahira (83-69) both improved by 14 strokes in the second round. The greatest improvement between successive rounds was 22 strokes achieved by Robin Davenport (94-72) in 1966 at Muirfield.

last two holes. "Today was probably one of the most fun rounds of golf I've ever played," McIlroy said. "It's strange to say that about battling to make the cut but I can leave with my head held high. I wanted to be here for the weekend. Selfishly, I wanted to feel that support for two more days."

McIlroy's inward run of 31 and his round of 65 both matched the best of the day. The other 65s came from South Africa's Justin Harding, who raced up to joint fifth on six-under-par, Xander Schauffele, one of the runners-up from Carnoustie in 2018, and Kevin Streelman, who improved by 12 strokes on his opening 77. For McIlroy, this was only the second time he had missed the cut in The Open. The last time it happened he returned to claim the Claret Jug at Royal Liverpool in 2014. So watch out Royal St George's in 2020.

Meanwhile, a new Champion Golfer seemed set to be crowned over the weekend at Portrush. The highest-ranked former winner at the halfway stage was Jordan Spieth at five-under-par after an adventurous 67. From the fifth hole, the Texan went birdie-birdie-eagle-birdie

Round of the Day: **Rory McIlroy – 65**

OFFICIAL SCORECARD
THE 148TH OPEN
ROYAL PORTRUSH

Rory MCILROY
Game 46
Friday 19 July at 3.10 pm

	FOR R&A USE ONLY		ROUND 2
18 HOLE TOTAL		79	36 HOLE TOTAL
THIS ROUND		65	144
36 HOLE TOTAL		144	

ROUND 2

Hole	1	2	3	4	5	6	7	8	9	Out	10	11	12	13	14	15	16	17	18	In	Total
Yards	421	574	177	482	174	194	592	434	432	3680	447	474	532	194	473	426	236	408	474	3664	7344
Par	4	5	3	4	4	3	5	4	4	36	4	4	5	3	4	4	3	4	4	35	71
Score	4	5	2	4		4	3	4	4	4	34	3	3	4	3	4	2	4	4		31	65

Signature of Marker

Signature of Player
Rory McIlroy

VERIFIED

After his calamity on Thursday at the 16th, McIlroy hits a majestic tee shot to 10 feet to set up a birdie.

An eagle-two for Adam Hadwin (left) at the eighth hole brought a high-five from Cameron Smith.

A 67 for Justin Rose to move two strokes off the lead.

Justin Harding surveys his putt at the 18th for a 65.

but at other times appeared intent on discovering hidden parts of the dunes. Far more steady was his fellow American Brooks Koepka, who birdied the 12th and 13th holes on the way to a 69 to be in the group sharing eighth place with Spieth.

A stroke better was Justin Rose, another of the runners-up from Carnoustie. The 2013 US Open champion was again showing the same silky putting touch he demonstrated for the first three days at Pebble Beach the previous month. An eagle at the 12th helped the Englishman to a 67 and six-under-par, alongside Harding and Australia's Cameron Smith, who had a 66.

Fleetwood briefly took the clubhouse lead at seven-under-par when the Southport man completed his own 67 with a birdie at the last. He described a round of six birdies and two bogeys as less "stress-free" than his bogey-free effort the

Tyrrell Hatton, who scored 71, drives at the 14th watched by Thomas Pieters and Keith Mitchell.

Jordan Spieth went five-under-par for four holes from the fifth on the way to a 67 for the 2017 Champion Golfer.

EXCERPTS FROM THE PRESS

"Elsewhere, JB Holmes, whose name sounds for all the world like a construction firm from south Derry, had built on his overnight advantage to move to eight-under, meaning McIlroy faced the prospect of starting his second round 16 shots off the lead, a gap as big as the Atlantic lapping onto the shore beneath the fifth green."

—Michael McWilliams,
The Irish News

"Padraig Harrington believes Shane Lowry's nightmare finish to the 2016 US Open at Oakmont can act as a help rather than a hindrance as the Offaly man chases a first major win at Portrush this weekend."

—Brendan O'Brien,
Irish Examiner

"Rory McIlroy had made such a hash of the first day of The Open that even making the cut at Royal Portrush would represent a victory."

—Rob Hodgetts,
CNN

"Tiger Woods told fans not to expect any miracles at this year's Open as he admitted the years are beginning to take their toll on his body."

—Adam Skinner,
Daily Express

Mythical creatures and local landmarks featured on Tommy Fleetwood's shirt.

Relief required: Denmark's Lucas Bjerregaard's ball became lodged under a seated spectator at the first hole.

previous day but was relishing being in contention at The Open again after going into the weekend with a chance at Carnoustie. Most eye-catching was his black-and-white shirt, apparently featuring golfers, the local landmarks and mythical creatures.

Discussion turned to a very real creature when Fleetwood said of Holmes: "I know he travels around America with his dog. I love that, a little bit jealous, to be honest."

While Fleetwood was speaking, Holmes birdied the 12th and 13th holes to go two ahead. He dropped a shot at the 14th and then parred in, which meant the overnight leader had maintained his position with a 68 to be eight-under-par. "That's two days in a row I've hit the ball really well and putted well," he said.

But that's not what the press wanted to know. Having been primed by Fleetwood, the conversation switched to Ace, a miniature golden doodle that Holmes bought in a charity auction and who has now become an inseparable part of the family.

Phil Mickelson, who missed the cut, in trouble at the 11th.

World number one Brooks Koepka unleashes a drive at the seventh hole during a steady second round of 69.

Dylan Frittelli leaps over the barriers by the 18th tee as he searched for his ball, unsuccessfully, at the 17th hole.

Westwood's winning combination?

In his 25th appearance at The Open, Lee Westwood cut a relaxed figure over the first two days of play. He had Helen Storey, his girlfriend, caddieing for him and the combination seemed to be reaping rich dividends for the former world number one.

The Englishman followed up a first round of 68 with one of 67, equalling his lowest at The Open, and he was quick to credit his caddie for her calming influence. "Helen doesn't know too much about golf but she knows a lot about the way my mind works, so she keeps me in a good frame of mind and focusing on the right things at the right time," he said. "There's more to caddieing than carrying the bag and getting the wind direction."

Westwood, who has a dry, mischievous sense of humour, offered a small insight into their working relationship. "You'd be surprised the sort of things we talk about out there," he said. "Dinner, where we're going on holiday, whether there's a nail file in the bag..." Among Helen's fears, he revealed, was picking up a divot with a worm in it. "I said I'd pick the shots off the top of the turf this week."

With five top-10 finishes, including once as runner-up, at The Open, Westwood had come close to lifting the game's most coveted trophy. Now, he said, he was no longer worried about success or failure. "I literally don't care," he claimed.

At which point, it was time to look for that pinch of salt.

Except for this week, when Ace stayed back in the States with Holmes' 18-month-old son, Tucker. Asked about trying to win on Tour, Holmes joked: "I'd prefer to go back to the dog questions."

Holmes' best result in a major came at The Open in 2016 when he was third at Royal Troon — or, to put it another way, he topped the leaderboard for mere mortals that week behind the runaway duel featuring Henrik Stenson and Mickelson.

Westwood had three top-three finishes in The Open and was now tied third again. The 46-year-old did not drop a stroke in a 67 that tied his best score in the Championship. All four of Westwood's birdies came in a back nine of 31, including at the 16th thanks to a putt of over 70 feet that he was just trying to get somewhere close to the hole. At the 17th he was in the rough but recovered to 15 feet and made that one as well. "It was a good solid day," he said. "I'm looking forward to putting my feet up this afternoon and catching a bit of golf."

He would have seen a lot of Lowry as the Irishman played catch-up. Every step of the way, he was cheered on by the gallery. The roar that greeted

the County Offaly man on the first tee was loud enough to make him smile, but those roars just kept getting louder. The 32-year-old was lapping up the atmosphere. He birdied the first. Then the second. Then the third, where he hit a seven-iron pin-high left of the flagstick and holed the putt from eight feet. "The crowd didn't seem so big around the third green but the roar there was unbelievable," Lowry said.

At the fifth he drove onto the sixth tee, just to the left of the fifth green, and then almost chipped in for eagle. At eight-under-par he was tied for the lead but a fifth birdie of the day at the eighth put him in front. Out in 31, Lowry then birdied the 10th with a long putt that was greeted with the loudest roar yet. "Incredible," Lowry marvelled. "You can but laugh. There's no point trying to shy away from it."

Perhaps it got to him a tad. Ten-under-par proved

Lowry acknowledges the fans on the 18th hole.

One final walk for teary Tom

With his exemption for winning The Open in 1996 expiring, Tom Lehman enjoyed one last walk up the 18th fairway, accompanied by his son, Thomas. "It was more emotional than I thought it would be," said the 60-year-old American. "I did everything in my power not to start bawling. I didn't totally succeed. It was very sweet and joyful … tears of joy."

Lehman revealed what he told his son: "I just said how much I loved him. There was nobody in the world I'd rather be walking down the fairway with right here than you. This may be my last one but maybe the next time

I'll be caddieing for you."

Recalling his triumph at Royal Lytham & St Annes, Lehman said he was accompanied all week wherever he went by a local police officer, Kevin Boyles. After helping Lehman through the spectators to get to the 18th

green, Boyles said: "Aye, Tom, we've been through a lot of **** together but now you're on your own."

"That's my favourite Open memory," Lehman said. "We switched hats after the thing was over. I've got one of his and he has one of my Dockers."

The following week Lehman crossed the Irish Sea to play in The Senior Open at Lytham, where he finished tied 36th. Before leaving Ireland, he said: "Listen, I could still win a Senior Open. I told my wife, if I could write the perfect script it would be to win next year so I get to play in The Open at St Andrews in 2021."

Holmes, whose dog Ace travels with him to tournaments in America, putts for a par at the 16th hole.

to be the high point of his round. Three putts at the 14th cost a shot. Then he got up and down at the next three holes. The 17th was eventful. On his drive he was disturbed at the top of his backswing by the commentary coming from a big screen at a spectator village near the 16th green. "I could hear Jay Townsend commentating on my shot, 'He's got 295 to the top of the hill'. Yeah, that put me off. But I got a good break and managed to make par."

His drive had finished in a position where he was able to get a free drop from the barriers around the 18th tee box. From an area where the grass had been trampled down by the spectators, Lowry played just over the green and then utilised his short game skills to seal a four. Others were not so lucky. Moments later Dylan Frittelli, who had got to eight-under-par with his fourth birdie in six holes at the 15th, lost his ball in a similar area and took a double-bogey. A bogey at the last

dropped the South African to five-under-par after a 69.

Lowry also dropped a stroke at the last when, as he freely admitted, he duffed his second shot and it came up short of the green. "I was trying to hit an eight-iron hard but got a bit tentative." It did not alter his feeling about the day. "There's not too many days like that on the golf course," he said. "I really enjoyed it and I'm really happy with where I am. Obviously, getting to 10-under-par, you are looking at keeping it there but that's two good days' work."

Although McIlroy led every day when he won in 2014, Harrington, Clarke and Paul McGinley can all attest that a 36-hole lead, or share, provides no guarantee. "I'm in a great position but, my God, have we got a long way to go. I need to go out and shoot the best round I can tomorrow and hopefully it leaves me in a good position into Sunday."

It seemed a good plan.

SECOND ROUND LEADERS

HOLE	1	2	3	4	5	6	7	8	9	10	11	12	13	14	15	16	17	18	TOTAL
PAR	4	5	3	4	4	3	5	4	4	4	4	4	5	3	4	4	3	4	4
JB Holmes	4	4	3	4	3	2	5	4	5	4	4	4	2	5	4	3	4	4	68-134
Shane Lowry	3	4	2	4	3	3	5	3	4	3	4	5	3	5	4	3	4	5	67-134
Tommy Fleetwood	5	4	3	4	3	3	5	4	4	4	4	4	2	4	3	4	4	3	67-135
Lee Westwood	4	5	4	4	4	3	5	4	4	4	4	4	2	4	4	2	3	4	67-135
Cameron Smith	4	4	3	4	4	3	4	3	5	3	4	4	2	4	4	3	4	4	66-136
Justin Harding	4	4	3	5	4	5	3	4	4	3	4	4	2	5	3	2	4	4	65-136
Justin Rose	4	4	3	5	4	3	4	4	3	4	4	3	3	4	4	3	4	4	67-136

■ EAGLE OR BETTER　■ BIRDIES　□ PAR　■ OVER PAR

SCORING SUMMARY

SECOND ROUND SCORES

Players Under Par	57
Players At Par	28
Players Over Par	71

LOW SCORES

Low First Nine

Shane Lowry	31

Low Second Nine

Jim Furyk	31
Justin Harding	31
Nate Lashley	31
Rory McIlroy	31
Xander Schauffele	31
Lee Westwood	31

Low Round

Justin Harding	65
Rory McIlroy	65
Xander Schauffele	65
Kevin Streelman	65

SECOND ROUND HOLE SUMMARY

HOLE	PAR	YARDS	EAGLES	BIRDIES	PARS	BOGEYS	D.BOGEYS	OTHER	RANK	AVERAGE
1	4	415	0	18	103	30	3	2	6	4.154
2	5	556	0	46	88	17	4	1	15	4.885
3	3	172	0	23	118	14	1	0	12	2.955
4	4	474	0	11	101	40	4	0	2	4.237
5	4	385	0	30	112	12	2	0	14	3.910
6	3	189	0	32	112	11	1	0	16	2.878
7	5	592	9	58	71	14	4	0	17	4.654
8	4	428	1	20	100	29	6	0	7	4.122
9	4	431	0	13	113	29	1	0	8	4.115
OUT	36	3,642	10	251	918	196	26	3		35.910
10	4	443	0	28	107	20	1	0	11	3.962
11	4	465	0	18	100	30	6	2	3	4.192
12	5	527	5	73	70	8	0	0	18	4.519
13	3	188	0	26	111	17	2	0	9	2.968
14	4	475	0	7	77	59	9	4	1	4.532
15	4	419	0	36	94	24	2	0	13	3.949
16	3	230	0	13	106	32	4	1	3	3.192
17	4	417	0	26	114	13	2	1	9	3.968
18	4	467	0	14	105	31	5	1	3	4.192
IN	35	3,631	5	241	884	234	31	9		35.474
TOTAL	71	7,273	15	492	1,802	430	57	12		71.385

> 66 Today I showed the real Rory McIlroy and the golf I can play. I'm leaving here with a pretty solid golf game. 99
>
> —Rory McIlroy

> 66 He's Rory McIlroy and I think nobody in the world of golf handles things better than him most of the time. 99
>
> —Tommy Fleetwood

> 66 Oh, my God, the crowd was incredible. They were so nice and respectful. The kids were respectful and that's not always the case when we travel around the world. 99
>
> —Tiger Woods

> 66 The goal was to make the cut and get the Silver Medal, so a bit disappointed, obviously. But that's golf. 99
>
> —James Sugrue

> 66 Playing partner doesn't shout 'fore'. The ball is going into the crowd. Just shout, simple as that. 99
>
> —Robert MacIntyre

> 66 I just grew up in the wind, having to play a lot of different shots and using imagination around the greens. So it's different but it feeds well into this style of golf. 99
>
> —Jordan Spieth

> 66 The rough is pretty brutal around the whole golf course, to be honest. Obviously, the aim is to stay out of it. Sadly, I didn't do that and I got punished. 99
>
> —Tyrrell Hatton

'Come on, Rory! We love you.'

Art Spander hears the adoration for McIlroy in his desperation to make the cut

His roots and memories were at Royal Portrush, the course he had visited as a lad and conquered as a teenager. And now Rory McIlroy of Holywood, Northern Ireland, was back, playing in The Open, playing for himself, playing for his country, playing with a sense of desperation.

An early stutter, finding sand at the second.

What happened that opening round, his very first shot sailing out of bounds in an eight-over-par total of 79, perhaps wouldn't have happened in a perfect scenario. But it did happen, golf at times being irritatingly imperfect.

So much attention — he had become the face of The Open; the favourite of The Open — so much hope and anticipation. Then so much gloom. "I didn't think it was going to be as bad as it was," he said. "But I'll dust myself off and come back and try to do better."

He did better, did what everyone knew Rory McIlroy could do. Hadn't he won an Open? Won a US Open? Won two US PGA Championships? He was no quitter. He had proved something to himself and to his fans.

He did plenty. He just didn't do enough. Breaking par doesn't necessarily keep a golfer from a broken heart.

But what a closing run on that second round. Birdies at 10, 11, 12, cheers rolling down the fairways, echoing in the bunkers, virtually carrying

McIlroy feels the love from his home fans.

to the Giant's Causeway down the Antrim Coast. A woman's voice pierced the air, "Come on, Rory! We love you."

Did Rory hear? Everybody there heard the collective "Oooh," when the par putt missed on 13. Then a birdie at 14, and another at 16. Just one more and the miracle would be complete. Just one more and Rory McIlroy, who had dreamed of this Open, would make the cut.

But links golf is wildly unpredictable, often a game of bounces. Jack Nicklaus, who won three Opens and 18 major championships overall, said, "The people who hit the best shots usually get the best bounces."

This time, Rory McIlroy got the bad bounce, his approach to the 18th green landing on a mound and spinning away. He leaned on his wedge, shook his head as if to say, "Not a chance," and with his left hand gestured the way he wanted the ball to go. His chip shot swerved beyond the cup. The tap-in par gave him a 31 on the homecoming nine, a 65 for the round, six-under-par, but one over the cut line.

Golf can be fickle. Fans need not be. Rory was their guy, the "homie," as the saying goes in America. The support never diminished from start to unhappy end.

"It's a moment I envisaged the last few years," said McIlroy of a tribute befitting a champion, which he is, just not the winner of what so many thought would be his Open. "It just happened two days early."

McIlroy, and the other major champions from Northern Ireland, Darren Clarke and Graeme McDowell, had led the successful attempt to return The Open to Royal Portrush after an absence of nearly 70 years.

"Portrush has been a very big — at least the golf club — has been a very big part of my upbringing," McIlroy said the day before The Open began. "I'm going to love being out there and having the crowds and the support. If that can't help you, nothing can."

He had that on his side, yet there's only so much the fans can do. The rest is up to the competitor. On Friday, the competitor performed the way those fans — and he — had wanted.

"I didn't play my part," McIlroy said apologetically. He meant on the scoreboard over the 36 holes. He meant as someone who wanted to be on the course all four rounds. Yet, truth tell, in actuality he did play his part, along with Clarke and McDowell, making the golf world, the entire sports world, understand how much the little nation at the tip of the Irish island had contributed to the game.

It didn't matter that McIlroy, as others, has a residence in Florida, enabling him to play the PGA Tour with a minimum of travel. Northern Ireland is home. "Sometimes you get so far away from all the people cheering you on back home, and you come back and play in front of them. It definitely hit me like a ton of bricks."

The Championship was hardly what McIlroy would have planned. And everything that he could have wanted. "I didn't know how people were going to react to my first round," he said, after his gallant play on Friday. "How many people were going to be on the first tee. Is it just a lost cause? But to have that many people out there following me, supporting me, cheering my name, it meant the world to me."

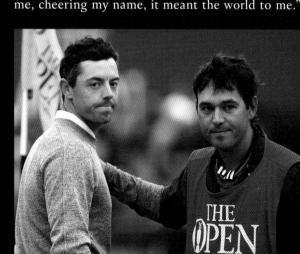

A consoling gesture from caddie Harry Diamond.

Lowry Takes Control

By Andy Farrell

If Friday was like a Sunday at The Open, then Saturday turned into a Sunday at the Ryder Cup when the home team is celebrating victory.

It was that loud, and almost that delirious, as Ireland's Shane Lowry took control of The 148th Open at Royal Portrush. "Ole, ole, ole," the crowd at the 18th hole chanted, along with other variants that incorporated Lowry's name, as the loveable giant of a golfer from Clara, County Offaly, marched towards a new course record of 63 for the revised Dunluce Links and a four-stroke lead.

"That's the most incredible day I've ever had on the golf course," said the 32-year-old Irishman. Walking off the 17th tee, Lowry said to his caddie, Brian "Bo" Martin: "We might never have a day like this on the golf course again. So let's enjoy the next half-hour." And they did. "The crowd was incredible. I can't believe what it was like.

"I thought I dealt with it very well today," Lowry

"The most incredible day" for leader Shane Lowry.

added. "Walking from the green to the next tee, people are literally a yard away from you roaring in your face as loud as they can. If you need to get up and hit a drive down a tight fairway, it's fairly difficult."

Yet Lowry was able to funnel their energy into golf of ever increasing brilliance. On Friday he had birdied six of the first 10 holes but fizzled out a bit over the closing stretch. On Saturday he started steadily, picked up a couple of shots and then birdied six of the last 10 holes.

It was easy to forget that for much of this third round, the leaderboard was relatively tightly packed. Early on there was a four-way tie for the lead. Lowry only got in front for good at the 12th. Going to the 15th he was only one in front. Suddenly he kicked clear of the field.

A drive and a wedge put him 12 feet away at the 15th hole. The putt curled from left to right and found the cup. Then came the shot of the day, possibly the Championship and even his life. From over 230 yards at the 16th hole, with the precipitous cliff on the right, Lowry struck a magnificent four-iron right on line with the hole, finishing 10 feet away.

Koepka's Open secret weapon

With a 1-2-1-2 run of results in his previous four major championships, Brooks Koepka came into The Open as the man to beat.

His not-so-secret secret weapon at Royal Portrush was the person carrying his bag. Ricky Elliott, who started caddieing for Koepka at the 2013 US PGA Championship, grew up playing at Portrush and brought intimate knowledge to the task in hand.

"There would be nothing cooler," Koepka said when asked what it would mean to Elliott if he were to win the Claret Jug. "I don't think when he grew up he thought there would ever be an Open Championship here. To be caddieing here and to win, he would be a legend. It would be cool to see him win."

Elliott certainly had plenty to offer. "It's a lot easier off the tee," Koepka said. "To know where the right spots to miss it, right spots to leave yourself on the greens, make it a little bit easier for me. He knows this golf course, and in every wind direction possible.

"Things change off the tee based on wind direction and hole location. So he knows exactly where to put it and tells me where to go and I fire it there."

Asked if his rivals would pay extra attention to his presence on the leaderboard after three rounds, Koepka played it cool: "I'm looking at the top spot, that's it. I'm assuming they probably do, but at the same time I have no idea."

Lowry rolls in the putt for a birdie at the 16th hole.

"I'm not to going to lie, I pushed it about five, 10 yards but it was a perfect four-iron," Lowry said. "I knew I couldn't go long. I knew if I pushed it on the flag it would make the carry. I decided to hit a little fade up the green and the moment it came off the club face I knew it was pretty close.

"And to roll the putt in was really nice." It never looked anywhere else. Another roar rang out across the sand dunes of the Dunluce Links. "Every time I had a putt today," he admitted, "I just wanted to hole it because I wanted to hear that roar. It was just incredible. An incredible day."

A third birdie in a row came at the 17th. Having driven into trouble at the same hole on Friday, this time his tee shot made it all the way down the hill to the semi-rough on the left-hand side. A pitch from 60 yards away finished four feet from the hole. A par at the last — his birdie putt for a 62 to equal Branden Grace's record low round set at Royal Birkdale in 2017 came up just short — and Lowry had set a new record of 197 strokes for the first 54 holes at The Open. Spoiler alert, if he won the following day, his 63 would become a new record for a Champion Golfer in the third round. For now, however, a golfer from the Republic of Ireland had sole possession of the lead with a round to play for the first time.

Brooks Koepka always threatened to catch fire but not enough putts dropped, as at the eighth hole.

Rickie Fowler walks off the fifth green with a birdie on the way to a 66. He came home in 31 strokes.

Xander Schauffele, here on the third tee, made up ground going out but a 69 left the American 11 strokes behind.

With Lowry at 16-under-par, lying second was Tommy Fleetwood on 12-under-par after his own bogey-free round of 66. More than his position, the Southport man was simply delighted to have been involved on such an occasion. "First of all, it was a very special day," Fleetwood said.

"A great day to be playing golf. Happy to be in the mix and play my part in the atmosphere today. People watching today, if they're not into golf after that ... I think it was amazing for the sport.

"The atmosphere for us as golfers was just great. I loved it. For or against you, you can't help but appreciate and love what today was and what tomorrow is going to be."

For much of the day Fleetwood was tied for the lead or within a stroke. He was still only one back with two to play yet walked off the 18th four behind. "Yeah, I know," he agreed with a disbelieving shake of the head. "I had a few chances and it would be easy to get frustrated but you have to look at it realistically. I had a great day. I had one of the best rounds of the day and I was bogey-free. Shane just played great and I'm four back. That's it. I'm happy how I played."

A great day for Tommy Fleetwood with a bogey-free 66.

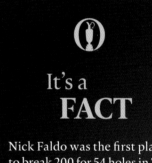

It's a
FACT

Nick Faldo was the first player to break 200 for 54 holes in The Open at St Andrews in 1990. He matched his own 199 total two years later at Muirfield, a mark also achieved by Adam Scott at Royal Lytham & St Annes in 2012 and Jordan Spieth at Royal Birkdale in 2017. Tom Lehman lowered the record to 198 at Lytham in 1996 before Shane Lowry's 197 at Royal Portrush in 2019.

Birdies at the last two holes gave Graeme McDowell a 68.

Playing alongside Lowry, his co-leader overnight JB Holmes was even closer to the epicentre of a seismic performance. "That was really cool to experience," said the American. "I'm happy for him, he played awesome.

"I don't know how many times in history you get the opportunity to witness that — to have someone from the home country put up a round like that in The Open. It's something I'll never forget.

"It wasn't my day," he added. "It wasn't like it was terrible. I played well, but when you're playing with a guy making everything, it feels like you shot a million." Briefly the solo leader after birdies at the second and third holes, it turned out to be Holmes under the hammer as Lowry forged a substantial lead. It took a birdie at the last for Holmes to retain outright third place, six strokes behind, one ahead of Brooks Koepka and Justin Rose.

A sunny but breezy morning made for tricky links conditions for

From sharing the lead overnight, JB Holmes finished six back.

After discussion with a Rules official, Lee Westwood accepted a penalty drop from a bush at the 10th hole.

Danny Willett, who had a 65, with caddie Sam Haywood.

those who had only just made the cut. Graeme McDowell entertained the fans with a 68, including birdies at the last two holes, the latter with a six-iron to two feet. Danny Willett posted a 65 that turned out to be only the second best score of the day. He was three off the lead when he finished but then the breeze died away and the 2016 Masters champion ended nine back alongside Jon Rahm, Jordan Spieth and Tony Finau. Chipping in from an awkward spot at the last saved Finau one if not, more likely, two strokes.

Once the leaders got on the course, it was Lee Westwood who made the first move with birdies at the second, third and fourth holes. A victory for the 46-year-old would have left him as the second oldest winner by a matter of days behind Old Tom Morris in 1867. Alas, the Worksop man had run out of birdies. He parred the rest of the front nine and then hit into a bush at the 10th.

Round of the Day: **Shane Lowry – 63**

OFFICIAL SCORECARD
THE 148TH OPEN
ROYAL PORTRUSH

Shane LOWRY
Game 37
Saturday 20 July at 3.50 pm

FOR R&A USE ONLY 37.1	ROUND 3
36 HOLE TOTAL 134	54 HOLE TOTAL
THIS ROUND ✓63	197 ✓
54 HOLE TOTAL ✓197	
VERIFIED GD	

ROUND 3

Hole	1	2	3	4	5	6	7	8	9	Out	10	11	12	13	14	15	16	17	18	In	Total
Yards	421	574	177	482	374	194	592	434	432	3680	447	474	532	194	473	426	236	408	474	3664	7344
Par	4	5	3	4	4	3	5	4	4	36	4	4	5	3	4	4	3	4	4	35	71
Score	4	5	(2)	4	(3)	3	5	4	(3)	33	(3)	4	(4)	3	4	(3)	(2)	(3)	4	30	63

Signature of Marker

Signature of Player — Shane Lowry

It was a plugged lie but Westwood readily agreed with a Rules official that the ball was unplayable so there was no question of a free drop. "I couldn't have played the shot even if it was sitting on a tee," he said. "I just accepted the penalty. I'm not interested in gaining an advantage in a situation like that. I could have faked it and said I would hit it left-handed over my shoulder but you let your conscience be your guide in situations like that."

The result was a bogey that was Westwood's first dropped shot since the 14th hole in the first round. Another followed with a three-putt at the 15th, so after a promising start he ended up with a 70. He was at eight-under-par, tied with Rickie Fowler, who made up ground with a 66, which included an inward half of 31.

Not all those in the final pairings scored well. Australia's Cameron Smith had a 71 and his playing partner Justin Harding a 74. The South African had been only one behind after two early birdies but his pitch shot at the fifth ran all the way through the clifftop green and finished an inch out of bounds. The hole had not been kind to Harding. On Thursday he had been plugged under the lip of a bunker and lost balance in attempting to escape. He posted a picture of himself beached in the sand on social media with the comment: "Golf is hard."

South Africa's Justin Harding fell back with a 74.

Shake on it: Robert MacIntyre, 71, Justin Thomas, 68.

EXCERPTS FROM THE PRESS

Justin Rose found the odd spot of trouble but returned a 68.

Rose flickered briefly with an 18-foot eagle putt at the 12th followed by two birdies in the next three holes to finish with a 68. Koepka always threatened to catch fire but only actually did so with birdies at the last two holes for a 67. The pair remained a long way behind the leader, with Koepka giving the impression that he was having one of those weeks when the putts burn the edges of the hole. The cold light of statistics, however, showed that Koepka had taken only one more putt to this point than leader Lowry. The American had hit six fewer greens in regulation than the Irishman, who notched 17 out of 18 on Saturday and 45 for the first three rounds.

After Fleetwood birdied the first hole from 15 feet, and Holmes the second and third holes, Lowry opened his account at the third from four feet. He then added a three at the fifth from six feet. Holmes got into trouble off the tee but saved his par.

Fleetwood had also birdied the fifth hole and added three more at the seventh, 10th and 12th holes. He got up and down at the 15th

Eric van Rooyen on missing a putt at the 18th hole.

Jon Rahm cannot believe this putt stayed out.

Jordan Spieth stayed in the top 10 with a 69.

A 68 for Tony Finau lifted the American to eighth.

Royal Portrush head professional Gary McNeill enjoyed his day as a marker for Paul Waring.

Host club pro Gary's perfect day

It is always an honour for the head professional of the host club to act as a marker in The Open when an odd number of players qualify for the weekend but especially so for Royal Portrush's Gary McNeill.

"I've been here as club pro for almost 20 years and when I started the idea of The Open coming back certainly wasn't on the cards," McNeill said. "To see it all come together and be part of it all, it's been incredible. It was a perfect Open day, sunshine, a bit of breeze, lovely."

McNeill had not played since Regional Qualifying at County Louth in June and it was only late on Friday evening that it was confirmed he would be required to accompany Paul Waring at 9.35am on Saturday. The club shop was briefly closed as all McNeill's assistants wanted to see their boss tee-off at the first. "I felt okay on the first tee but as soon as I took the club back it felt foreign," he said.

"Paul was lovely to play with and it was great fun. There were so many members and friends out there and the reception the players are getting is unbelievable, they must be having a ball." A monster putt holed at the 17th and a solid par at the last were the highlights of the 49-year-old's day. "I've been to lots of Opens and sat in the grandstands watching the players coming up the 18th, but to actually experience it was quite a moment."

Holmes plays from a bunker at the seventh hole but failed to get up and down for a birdie.

for a par but missed further chances of birdies at the 11th, 14th and 17th holes. The importance of those misses grew the further Lowry went ahead.

Holmes parred his way to the 11th before claiming a birdie at the 12th hole. But he three-putted the next and could not save himself from a bunker at the 14th. By now Lowry was in full flow. He birdied the ninth with an eight-iron to 10 feet to go out in 33.

Then, from the rough at the 10th, his caddie talked him into taking advantage of the mounds to the left of the green and his seven-iron approach swung obligingly round to eight feet. Another birdie, another roar. A six-iron for his second found the green at the 12th and he two-putted for his four. Another bit of luck came at the 14th when a wild drive hit the neck of a spectator and came to rest with a playable lie in the dunes.

His second came up short but he got up and

Westwood and Fleetwood enjoyed their day together.

Lowry receives a thunderous ovation at the 18th hole after a par gave him a new course record.

down for a par. The almighty finish that followed gave him a second nine of 30 and advanced knowledge of the cross examination to follow. The word "Oakmont" had barely left an interviewer's lips when he said: "I was waiting for that. I said to Bo when I looked at the leaderboard and saw I was four ahead, 'At least I won't have to answer any questions about Oakmont.'"

At the 2016 US Open, when the third round was completed on the Sunday morning, Lowry was four ahead. An uncomfortable six-hour wait followed before a closing 76 left him in a share of second place. Arguably the uncertainty surrounding Dustin Johnson's standing, due to a Rules issue that was only confirmed after the round, affected the Irishman more than the American.

"I learned a lot about myself at Oakmont," Lowry said. "I learned that playing in the last round of a major with the lead you need to hang in there to the very last minute. You never know what can happen."

"But that's a long time ago," he added. Following that defeat he got married and now has a two-year-old daughter. "I feel like a different person. I don't think I'm much of a different golfer but it probably doesn't mean as much to me as it did then. I've got a family now. No matter what I shoot tomorrow, they will be waiting for me.

"Tomorrow is a huge day in my career. It's weird to say it doesn't mean as much because it's not far off. You know what I'm saying ... I don't really know what I'm saying, to be honest. It's been a long day, lads."

You knew what he meant. It meant everything, and all Ireland expected, but Wendy and Iris would be there anyway, which meant more.

THIRD ROUND LEADERS

HOLE	1	2	3	4	5	6	7	8	9	10	11	12	13	14	15	16	17	18	
PAR	4	5	3	4	4	3	5	4	4	4	4	5	3	4	4	3	4	4	TOTAL
Shane Lowry	4	5	2	4	3	3	5	4	3	3	4	4	3	4	3	2	3	4	63-197
Tommy Fleetwood	3	5	3	4	3	3	4	4	4	3	4	4	3	4	4	3	4	4	66-201
JB Holmes	4	4	2	4	4	3	5	4	4	4	4	4	4	5	4	3	4	3	69-203
Brooks Koepka	4	4	3	4	4	3	4	4	4	4	4	4	3	5	3	3	3	3	67-204
Justin Rose	4	4	3	4	4	3	5	5	4	4	4	3	2	4	3	4	4	4	68-204
Rickie Fowler	4	5	3	5	3	3	4	4	4	3	3	5	3	4	3	3	3	4	66-205
Lee Westwood	4	4	2	3	4	3	5	4	4	5	4	5	3	4	5	3	4	4	70-205

■ EAGLE OR BETTER   ■ BIRDIES   ☐ PAR   ■ OVER PAR

SCORING SUMMARY

THIRD ROUND SCORES

Players Under Par	30
Players At Par	16
Players Over Par	27

LOW SCORES

Low First Nine

Byeong Hun An	33
Tony Finau	33
Tommy Fleetwood	33
Shane Lowry	33
Sang Hyun Park	33
Xander Schauffele	33
Henrik Stenson	33
Justin Thomas	33
Lee Westwood	33
Danny Willett	33

Low Second Nine

Shane Lowry	30

Low Round

Shane Lowry	63

THIRD ROUND HOLE SUMMARY

HOLE	PAR	YARDS	EAGLES	BIRDIES	PARS	BOGEYS	D.BOGEYS	OTHER	RANK	AVERAGE
1	4	422	0	4	60	8	1	0	8	4.082
2	5	570	2	47	22	2	0	0	18	4.329
3	3	169	0	15	50	8	0	0	15	2.904
4	4	487	0	9	47	14	3	0	5	4.151
5	4	386	0	16	49	4	3	1	13	3.959
6	3	205	0	1	54	17	1	0	3	3.247
7	5	577	1	15	45	12	0	0	14	4.932
8	4	440	0	16	44	12	1	0	12	3.973
9	4	422	0	10	53	10	0	0	10	4.000
OUT	36	3,678	3	133	424	87	9	1		35.575
10	4	450	0	13	48	11	1	0	10	4.000
11	4	464	0	7	41	21	3	1	2	4.315
12	5	522	2	34	34	3	0	0	17	4.521
13	3	178	0	9	50	14	0	0	9	3.068
14	4	478	0	7	39	24	2	1	1	4.329
15	4	434	0	10	47	14	2	0	6	4.110
16	3	232	0	2	51	20	0	0	3	3.247
17	4	406	0	22	43	8	0	0	16	3.808
18	4	481	0	9	49	14	1	0	7	4.096
IN	35	3,645	2	113	402	129	9	2		35.493
TOTAL	71	7,323	5	246	826	216	18	3		71.068

❝ I'll go to bed thinking about holding the Claret Jug tomorrow evening. It's only natural, isn't it? We're human. We're not robots. **❞**

—Shane Lowry

❝ It's definitely not over yet. If he plays like that again it's over. But a lot can happen. I put myself in a good position, go out there tomorrow and keep trucking. **❞**

—JB Holmes

❝ I've had my fair share of support for the first three days. Hopefully, there will still be some people out there rooting for me tomorrow. **❞**

—Tommy Fleetwood

❝ It's never not fun to shoot 65 on Saturday at The Open. **❞**

—Danny Willett

❝ When you get to the weekend of a major championship it goes so quickly. Playing two balls, the rounds go so fast. **❞**

—Lee Westwood

❝ Nobody has hit it better than me this week. I've hit it as good as I could possibly imagine. I putted the worst in the entire field. **❞**

—Brooks Koepka

❝ I got just about enough out of the day that I needed to sort of stay in contention. **❞**

—Justin Rose

❝ You've got to take what you get with the weather. Go throw the waterproofs on and have fun. That's links golf. That's The Open. **❞**

—Rickie Fowler

Chorus of approval for a proper links

The world's best players fall in love with Royal Portrush, writes Alistair Tait

No decision has been taken on The Open's return to Royal Portrush. The world's top players say it should be sooner rather than later. Unanimously.

It's unusual to gather 156 golfers and not hear at least one complaint about the golf course. It happened at The 148th Open. The 7,344-yard, par 71 Dunluce Links emerged from this Open with top marks.

"The greatest compliment is that all the feedback I've heard from the players has been positive and, especially on a links course, that's not something you often hear," said defending Champion Golfer Francesco Molinari.

Scores over the first two rounds ranged from 65 to a freakish David Duval 91 thanks to a comedy of errors at the seventh hole in round one. Take Duval's anomaly out of the picture and the worst score was 83. That 65-83 range was about right given testing conditions of wind and rain over the opening two rounds.

Competitors turned up on Saturday to find Royal Portrush in a more convivial mood. No wind, no rain, just perfect conditions ideal for scoring. Shane Lowry returned a course-record 63 to take control of the Championship. Four players posted a 77, the highest score of the day.

"We got very lucky with the weather," Lowry admitted. "The wind laid down and it played quite easy towards the end. The greens are perfect and we're playing links golf in no wind. It virtually had no real protection out there. If you were hitting decent shots you were getting good results. That's what happened today."

As far as local boy Graeme McDowell was concerned, Royal Portrush in different conditions was just what The 148th Open needed.

"The golf course has been phenomenal," McDowell said. "We've seen flat, calm conditions, we've seen wind directions changing all week. You could say they've seen a lot of Portrush. They've seen a lot of what this golf course can offer."

Like Molinari, McDowell received nothing but positive comments from his peers when he quizzed them about the course on which he learned to play the game as a member of Rathmore Golf Club, near the main entrance to this year's Championship.

"They just love the golf course," McDowell said. "They feel like it's the best links they've ever seen. I think the balance this golf course has, it's all there in front of you. It's got length, it's got some short holes. It's got some quirkiness in places. But it's all there. It's very fair.

"Caddies and players and some of the commentating crew out there, people are saying it's just one of the best links they've ever seen. Which is high praise from the best players in the world who get to play the best courses on the planet."

Jim Furyk was playing in The Open for the 22nd time, enough to have played every venue in the pool of courses used for the game's oldest major.

"I like the golf course," Furyk said. "I don't think it suited any particular style. I felt like

The cliffs of Whiterocks form a stunning backdrop at Royal Portrush as fans watch from the tee at the new seventh hole.

t gave everyone a chance to play. It was mostly straightforward. There are some blind shots, some hidden humps and bumps, but you could figure out the golf course pretty quickly.

"If I can steal an Irish term, it's a 'proper links'."

Paul Casey participated in his 17th Open. Like Furyk, he has played every Open course. He also has vast experience of links golf from his amateur days. He knows the capricious nature, the luck of the bounce, of links golf that often determines a player's score. Yet he walked off Royal Portrush feeling as if the scores he posted were down to him, and nothing to do with luck.

"I never really think links golf is fair, but this course is pretty close," Casey said. "It's as good as it gets. I would like to see the course used again on the Open rota very soon.

"From the golf course and the crowds alone, why would you not come back? It's already been a massive success. This course should definitely have another Open soon."

Jordan Spieth returned scores of 70, 67 and 69 to head into the final round in joint eighth place. He shot 77 in the brutal conditions of the final round to finish equal 20th. Spieth's sad Sunday didn't affect his opinion of the golf course.

"It was amazing," said the 2017 Champion Golfer. "I hope it's on the rotation. I enjoyed the golf course. It played tough and fair. It was scorable yesterday, and maybe the afternoon before. Today it was really really tough and showed its teeth."

If there were doubts about Royal Portrush's return to major championship golf, this Open dispelled them. Suffice it to say, it will be a lot less than 68 years before The Open comes back to Northern Ireland. How about six to eight years?

Lowry Shares The Open Joy

By Andy Farrell

The roars, the chants, the tears, the hugs, the smiles, the arms open wide in celebration. Was there ever a more joyous reception for a winner at The Open?

Peter Alliss, one of the few people alive who played at Royal Portrush 68 years earlier, thought not. Shane Lowry, the latest Champion Golfer of the Year from Ireland, deserved every moment of it. And so, too, did all those who made The 148th Open such a triumphant return to the Antrim coast.

It was the ending all Ireland were hoping for and all Ireland appeared to be on hand to witness Lowry's victory in person. This was an "I was there" moment for Irish golf and how many will claim just that in the decades ahead?

The scale of the occasion gave this final day a tension over and above that of the sporting contest that played out on the Dunluce Links. The scorecards show that Lowry's playing partner, England's Tommy Fleetwood, was never closer

Shane Lowry with his prize, the Claret Jug.

than three behind Lowry and after three holes never closer than four.

The weather made it almost impossible for the chasers to mount a sustained challenge but they were waiting should Lowry falter at the top of the leaderboard. There was a wobble at the first hole, another in the middle of the round when the conditions were at their foulest, but on marched Clara's finest, a bearded bear of a man, seemingly impervious to the cold and rain in a short-sleeve shirt and sleeveless gilet.

Finally, there came the birdie at the 15th hole and a roar to match those of Saturday evening's exploits. He won by six strokes from Fleetwood, eight from Tony Finau and nine from Lee Westwood and the world number one Brooks Koepka. But only at the 72nd hole did the tension turn to the tumult of Ireland celebrating its newest favourite son.

Even then Lowry had difficulty in taking it all in. "I couldn't believe it was happening to me," said the 32-year-old with a natural self-effacement. "I thought about it all day but I didn't really let myself think about it until I hit my tee shot on 17. As soon as I hit that tee shot, I knew I couldn't really lose a ball from there.

A first birdie of the day arrived at the fourth hole for Lowry.

"I hit my tee shot on 18 and that was it. I started to enjoy it then. I tried to soak it in as much as I could but it was hard to, it was such a surreal experience. So many people wanted me to win. And then I walked round the corner and could see all my family and friends at the back of the green. To be honest, I welled up a bit and Bo told me to catch hold of myself, I still had to hit a shot. Thankfully, I hit a decent shot in there and two-putted."

Brian "Bo" Martin, his caddie from Ardglass, Northern Ireland, had been at Lowry's side for the previous 10 months and was never needed more than on this momentous day. "He was unbelievable today," Lowry said. "He kept on my back all day, kept talking to me, kept in my ear, kept me in the moment. I kept telling him how nervous I was, how scared I was, how much I didn't want to mess it up — all I could think about was walking down 18 with a four- or five-shot lead. And luckily I got to do that."

Martin got the first bearhug when it was all over. "I've known Bo a long time and now he's become a good friend of mine. To be able to share it with someone so close was very special."

A missed birdie putt at the first hole set the tone for Tommy Fleetwood.

The agonies for JB Holmes continued to the final hole as the early Championship front-runner concluded with an 87.

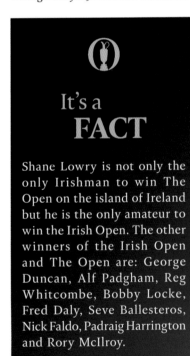

It's a
FACT

Shane Lowry is not only the only Irishman to win The Open on the island of Ireland but he is the only amateur to win the Irish Open. The other winners of the Irish Open and The Open are: George Duncan, Alf Padgham, Reg Whitcombe, Bobby Locke, Fred Daly, Seve Ballesteros, Nick Faldo, Padraig Harrington and Rory McIlroy.

Next came wife Wendy and daughter Iris, in her miniature *Keeping Faith* yellow raincoat. They have always kept the faith. They were there in Abu Dhabi when Lowry won for the first time in almost four years, but they would have been there anyway, win or lose. "My wife knew, no matter what, to have her there waiting for me," said Lowry of his daughter, "because if things didn't go to plan, at least she would have consoled me a little bit. To have her here and winning, obviously it's very special."

Parents Brendan, an All-Ireland Gaelic football champion, and Brigid were next, followed by coach Neil Manchip, whose chats, especially the confidence-boosting one over coffee on Wednesday, meant even more than the technical assistance. "I didn't even know going out this morning if I was good enough to win a major," Lowry admitted. "I tried to give my best, but it helped an awful lot that people around me really believed that I could. Neil always said that I was going to win one, at least one. And look, now here I am, a major champion. I can't believe I'm saying it."

Lowry had joined the ranks of the Irish major winners and, along

Tony Finau, with a 71, finished third, his best result in a major.

Bogeys at the first four holes for a shocked Brooks Koepka.

Lowry was seemingly impervious to the cold and rain.

with Gary Murphy, a friend from his first days on the European Tour, there were Graeme McDowell and Padraig Harrington, the two-time Champion Golfer who came back especially after missing the cut, waiting their turn to offer congratulations at the back of the 18th green.

"I think Paddy paved the way for the success of Irish golfers and I'm so happy I can add my name to the list of major champions," Lowry said. "But I used to curse them an awful lot in the past because that's all anybody wanted to know about in Ireland because they were winning so many majors. 'When are you going to win one?' Winning regular events wasn't good enough for anyone."

Lowry had never been a prolific winner. He did win the North of Ireland Amateur at Royal Portrush in 2008 and the following year, in similarly rainy conditions to here, became the only ever amateur winner of the Irish Open. He turned professional the following week but had to wait until the Portugal Masters in 2012 to cash his first winner's cheque. It was three years again before he won the WGC Bridgestone Invitational. If he didn't win often, he at least won big.

Lee Westwood held steady to take fourth place with Koepka.

"We expected gremlins to be unleashed and for Lowry to be tested like never before, but the man from County Offaly was never less than three shots clear of the field."

—Rick Broadbent,
The Times

"A year at the majors that began with one perfect storyline in Tiger Woods' victory at Augusta had ended in another, and the most passionate moment yet in Ireland's all-consuming love affair with golf."

—Derek Lawrenson,
Daily Mail

"It is, and will always be, the stuff of delight that we Clara folk belong to the same geographical tribe as this wonderful new Champion."

—Eddie Cunningham,
Irish Independent

"Even in the pin-rattling wind and the heavy rain that often seemed to be falling horizontally, Shane Lowry made winning his first major championship look as natural and easy as his light-up-the-clubhouse grin."

—Christopher Clarey,
The New York Times

"Irish golf has so much to celebrate — not just producing a new major champion in Shane Lowry but also the resounding success of The Open's return to Royal Portrush."

—Iain Carter,
BBC Sport

Fleetwood could not put pressure on Lowry early in the round but still finished as runner-up.

Fleetwood keeps his dream alive

Tommy Fleetwood made little attempt to hide his pain at finishing runner-up to Shane Lowry at Royal Portrush.

"I'm obviously disappointed and a bit low," the popular Englishman said. "It's my dream to win The Open and it always will be. It feels a lot rougher when you've come so close to what you've dreamt as a kid."

Fleetwood, who started the day four strokes behind Lowry, missed several chances early in the round to close the gap on the Irishman. It was, he said, his failure to "convert the putts" and a poor job in fixing "errant shots" that cost him dear. He did, however, take heart from his overall performance. This was the second time he had finished runner-up at a major — the other time was the US Open in 2018 — and he knows he has the game to go one better.

"That's the first time I've played in the last group of a major on a Sunday," he said. "For four rounds of golf I was the second-best player in the event, which is a great achievement. You have to look at it like that. I'm sure in a few hours, or a couple of days, I might see that.

"I'm trending in the right way and I just hope my time will come eventually. You can reflect all you want when you finish 30th or 40th, but it's these kinds of results that you look at and you know that you can find more in. Hopefully I'll put myself in position again."

Justin Thomas chips at the fifth hole, where he made a birdie on the way to a 72 and 11th place.

Yet at The Open at Carnoustie in 2018 he missed the cut for the fourth successive year — so much for the promise of a ninth-place finish on his third appearance in 2014. "I sat in the car park in Carnoustie on the Thursday, a year ago this week, and I cried," Lowry admitted. "Golf wasn't my friend at the time. It was something that was very stressful and it was weighing on me and I just didn't like doing it. What a difference a year makes, I suppose."

In September, he hired Martin as his caddie. In January 2019, he won the Abu Dhabi HSBC Championship. He led by three overnight, was four behind with seven to play, and birdied the last to win by one. He was eighth at the PGA Championship at Bethpage and then runner-up at the RBC Canadian Open, where Rory McIlroy won and McDowell also celebrated securing a place in his hometown Open.

A sixth-place finish for Rickie Fowler.

Lowry hit his approach at the 15th hole to eight feet (opposite page) and then holed the putt to go six strokes ahead.

This was an Open that Lowry had won on Saturday night but could still lose on a wild Sunday. Tee-times were moved up by an hour due to the forecast, which suited the leader since he woke at 6am, well short of his usual eight to 10 hours' sleep. The early starters actually had a pleasant round, with Francesco Molinari concluding the defence of his title with a best-of-the-day 66.

Young Scottish left-hander Robert MacIntyre scored a 68 to jump into a tie for sixth place. He was the first Scot to finish in the top 10 at The Open since Colin Montgomerie was runner-up to Tiger Woods at St Andrews in 2005. MacIntyre was also the first Scot to be in the top 10 on his debut since amateur Robert Reid Jack in 1959. Also finishing sixth was Tyrrell Hatton, who teed-off two hours before the leaders and was the last player to break par with a 69, as well as Danny Willett and Rickie Fowler. The American, only an orange cap of his usual last-day outfit visible under the waterproofs, went out of bounds at the first on the way to a 74.

He was not the only one. JB Holmes, leader for the first two days, also had to reload at the first. For the first three rounds, no one had hit more fairways than Holmes. On Sunday, no one hit fewer. He found the short grass only three times on the way to four double-bogeys and a triple in an 87 that was the worst score of the day by seven strokes and the highest in the final round of The Open since 1966.

Lowry had probably not seen either of Fowler's or Holmes' efforts at the first, but his history with the course meant he was fully aware of the out of bounds — his opponent in the final of the North of Ireland Amateur had found it 11 years earlier. After the customary huge cheer, Lowry's smile to the gallery was tight-lipped and the nerves were betrayed by a pulled two-iron that fortunately did not have enough on it to reach the white line.

Justin Rose, a runner-up in 2018, fell down the leaderboard with an uncharacteristic closing round of 79.

A 73 for Danny Willett to finish tied for sixth place.

"I had a nice healthy lead and hit a ropy tee shot on the first," Lowry said. "I actually hit a decent second." The four-iron from the rough found a bunker short of the raised green and he came out to 40 feet. His first putt stopped eight feet short of the hole.

Meanwhile, Fleetwood had hit two fine shots to 10 feet. A three-shot swing was in the offing, but the Englishman saw his birdie attempt dribble wide while Lowry buried his bogey putt. It was a shot lost but it could have been far worse, already a vital moment in the day. "That settled me an awful lot," Lowry said.

A tone had been set, at least as far as Fleetwood's putting was concerned. He missed chances for birdie on the second, for par on the third, for birdie from longish range at the fourth when the ball stopped only a roll short, and for eagle on the fifth. Not until getting up and down at the sixth did he one-putt. "Those first few holes, when you

'Proud of Portrush and all Ireland'

As the only Northern Irishman to make the cut, Graeme McDowell was ensured of a rousing ovation even as he closed with a 77 while finishing in the worst of the weather. "I'm not going to let that spoil my week," said the 2010 US Open champion. "It's been special. I've enjoyed every second and I'm really, really proud."

McDowell, an honorary member at Royal Portrush, who learnt his golf playing on the Valley and Dunluce Links as a member of the Rathmore club, added: "I'm proud of Portrush, proud of Northern Ireland and I'm proud of all Ireland.

"I'm probably most proud of the atmosphere created by the crowds. The people have been amazing, they've supported all the players and treated everyone like one of their own. Saturday, I was walking up the first hole at 10am and they were 10 deep. It was like a Ryder Cup. Today, walking up 18, the rain was coming in but the people still were amazing. They haven't let us down in any way, shape or form.

"The R&A have done a phenomenal job for the players and families, and everyone involved. The golf course has been phenomenal. It has been incredibly well presented and everyone is telling me this is their favourite Open venue. So many ticks in all the right boxes.

"We knew this was going to be a special Open. To have an Irishman at the top of the leaderboard is extra, extra special. Hopefully, we can come back soon."

Fleetwood got out of position at the 14th hole and after a double-bogey it was "pretty much over".

POS		TOT	HOLE	RND	POS		TOT	HOLE	RND
1	LOWRY, Shane	-15	15	+1	T6	MACINTYRE, Robert	-5	18	-3
2	FLEETWOOD, Tommy	-9	15	+3	T6	HATTON, Tyrrell	-5	18	-2
T3	FINAU, Tony	-7	18	E	T6	WILLETT, Danny	-5	18	+2
T3	KOEPKA, Brooks	-7	16	+2	T6	FOWLER, Rickie	-5	17	+3
5	WESTWOOD, Lee	-6	18	+2	10	REED, Patrick	-4	18	E

With Lowry six ahead, fans craned to get any view they could of the new Champion Golfer of the Year.

Francesco Molinari, the 2018 Champion Golfer of the Year, finished in style with the low round of the day, a 66.

Round of the Day: **Shane Lowry – 72**

OFFICIAL SCORECARD
THE 148TH OPEN
ROYAL PORTRUSH

Shane LOWRY ✓✓
Game 37
Sunday 21 July at 1.47 pm

	FOR R&A USE ONLY 37.2	ROUND 4
54 HOLE TOTAL	197	72 HOLE TOTAL
THIS ROUND	72	
72 HOLE TOTAL	269	269
VERIFIED	SrG	

ROUND 4

Hole	1	2	3	4	5	6	7	8	9	Out	10	11	12	13	14	15	16	17	18	In	Total
Yards	421	574	177	482	374	194	592	434	432	3680	447	474	532	194	473	426	236	408	474	3664	7344
Par	4	5	3	4	4	3	5	4	4	36	4	4	5	3	4	4	3	4	4	35	71
Score	5	5	3	3	3	3	4	5	5	36	4	5	5	3	5	3	3	4	4	36	72

Signature of Marker

Signature of Player: Shane Lowry

start four back, were pretty crucial," Fleetwood said. "I didn't do a good enough job of pressing at that point."

Nor was anyone else, although Westwood, after missing a tiddler at the first, birdied three of the next four holes to get within five. He got no closer and came home in 38 for a 73. He was delighted with a fourth place that earned him another trip to the Masters Tournament and a 26th appearance in The Open at Royal St George's in 2020. "I always feel I can perform at The Open," he said.

"It doesn't just suit one style of play. You don't have to be a bomber, which I'm probably not any more, you've just got to have cunning and guile, know how to get your ball round, especially when it gets like this."

It was getting wetter and windier. Surprisingly, although something similar happened on the last day of the US Open at Pebble Beach, Justin Rose crashed to a 79, while, perhaps even more surprising, Koepka opened with four straight bogeys. The American got two back with an eagle at the fifth but could never mount a charge. He ended with a 74, some 13 shots better than his playing partner Holmes, to end his run of four successive top two finishes in majors.

He did become only the fourth player to finish in the top four at all four majors in one year, after Jack Nicklaus in 1973, Tiger Woods in 2005 and Jordan Spieth in 2015. "It wasn't the finish I was looking for," Koepka said. "It was a great run for three of them. I'll try and improve for next year." Steady on, he was already 22 strokes better than anyone else in the majors in 2019.

Lowry birdied the fourth and fifth holes from eight feet and then got his four at the seventh to go up by six strokes. The worst of the weather hit on the next hole and led to a run of three bogeys in four holes. Lowry saw from Fleetwood's dropped shots at the eighth and the 10th, and from looking at the scoreboards, that no one was finding it easy. Fleetwood's birdie from 20 feet at the 12th got him within four, but after Lowry had saved par from a bunker at the 13th — he never dropped a shot at Portrush's stout collection of par threes all week — it was the 14th which ended the Englishman's hopes.

He drove into a bunker and, in trying to do too much by way of recovery, ended up in the rough on a hillock short of the green. His third ran off the green and a double-bogey was the result. "That was the killer," Fleetwood said. "It's such a difficult hole if you get out of position but I clearly made a mess of it. You don't want to think it, but it was pretty much over."

Lowry bogeyed the hole after missing the green but birdied the next from eight feet and that was

Fighting "until the bitter end", Lowry plays his approach at the last hole knowing victory was within his grasp.

The shortest putt to win the biggest prize, a Claret Jug.

that. "It was brutal out there at times and that makes Shane's one-over-par round even more impressive," said Fleetwood. "He controlled the tournament from the start to the end and that's a very impressive thing to do."

Fleetwood, who was also runner-up at the US Open in 2018, ended with a 74 and Lowry a 72 for a 15-under-par total of 269. Five players started the day with a chance of recording four rounds in the 60s — Lowry, Fleetwood, Koepka, Rose and Holmes — and none did so. The only player to match par from the last 10 pairings was Finau, who quietly snuck up into third place, his best result in a major. "I was just happy with the way I hung in there," said the man from Utah, who also finished in the top 10 at Carnoustie. "I knew winning the Championship was out of my grasp but I wanted to keep fighting to post as good a number as I could."

"Such a surreal experience, so many people wanted me to win." Finally, the celebrations could begin for Lowry.

That had been the lesson Lowry learnt from losing a four-stroke lead with a round to play at the 2016 US Open. "I knew I had to fight until the bitter end today," he said. "That's where I struggled at Oakmont. I'd give anything to have those last four holes back. Today, I thought I played the last five holes incredibly well. Links golf, bunkers, rough, all sorts can happen. I let myself enjoy it going down 18 but before that I was really fighting."

And then came the celebrations. A final question asked about future triumphs. "Geez," Lowry interrupted, "let me enjoy this one." And so he did, from the pubs of Dublin to a parade in Clara and an appearance at Croke Park, the home of Gaelic sport.

Good on him. The lasting image of Portrush is of the big fella with his arms outstretched, sharing the joy with all.

He is that kind of man. It was that kind of Open.

Wife Wendy and daughter Iris greet the Champion Golfer.

> " It's huge for Irish golf and for Irish sport. I'd say there were people that watched golf today that never watched golf before. "
>
> —Shane Lowry

> " You learn things as you go. I watched Shane win The Open. I watched how he conducted himself and how he played. "
>
> —Tommy Fleetwood

> " I would say the shot I was most proud of today was the second tee ball off the first. It's never fun hitting another after going OB. "
>
> —Rickie Fowler

> " I hit a six-iron from 145 yards at the 17th, leaned on it way too much and shanked it straight into the crowd. Not the way we wanted to finish. "
>
> —Henrik Stenson

> " It's been an interesting week. It gave me a sense of closure coming back. It's never easy to defend, especially in a major. Hopefully next time I'll be mentally more ready to defend another major. "
>
> —Francesco Molinari

> " Highlight of the week was holing a 20-footer on 18 there. The hair is standing on the back of your neck when that putt goes in. That's what you play the game for. "
>
> —Robert MacIntyre

> " We've played in worse rain. We've played in more wind. Yes, it was on the biggest stage on a demanding course but it was still doable. "
>
> —Russell Knox

FOURTH ROUND LEADERS

HOLE	1	2	3	4	5	6	7	8	9	10	11	12	13	14	15	16	17	18	
PAR	4	5	3	4	4	3	5	4	4	4	4	5	3	4	4	3	4	4	TOTAL
Shane Lowry	5	5	3	3	3	3	4	5	5	4	5	5	3	5	3	3	4	4	72-269
Tommy Fleetwood	4	5	4	4	3	3	5	5	4	5	4	4	3	6	4	3	4	4	74-275
Tony Finau	4	5	3	4	4	3	4	4	4	5	4	4	4	4	4	3	4	4	71-277
Lee Westwood	5	4	2	4	3	3	5	4	5	3	5	5	3	6	4	4	4	4	73-278
Brooks Koepka	5	6	4	5	2	3	5	4	4	4	5	5	3	5	4	3	5	4	74-278

■ EAGLE OR BETTER   ■ BIRDIES   □ PAR   ■ OVER PAR

SCORING SUMMARY

FOURTH ROUND SCORES

Players Under Par	15
Players At Par	11
Players Over Par	47

CHAMPIONSHIP SCORES

Rounds Under Par	143
Rounds At Par	67
Rounds Over Par	248

LOW SCORES

Low First Nine

Jason Kokrak	33
Doc Redman	33
Justin Thomas	33

Low Second Nine

Francesco Molinari	32

Low Round

Francesco Molinari	66

FOURTH ROUND HOLE SUMMARY

HOLE	PAR	YARDS	EAGLES	BIRDIES	PARS	BOGEYS	D.BOGEYS	OTHER	RANK	AVERAGE
1	4	430	0	6	44	16	6	1	5	4.342
2	5	581	2	24	42	5	0	0	18	4.685
3	3	180	0	12	50	11	0	0	14	2.986
4	4	489	0	9	48	16	0	0	11	4.096
5	4	376	2	30	33	5	2	1	17	3.699
6	3	174	0	7	57	9	0	0	12	3.027
7	5	586	1	28	35	7	2	0	16	4.740
8	4	434	0	4	46	20	2	1	6	4.315
9	4	436	0	4	41	26	2	0	4	4.356
OUT	**36**	**3,686**	**5**	**124**	**396**	**115**	**14**	**3**		**36.247**
10	4	462	0	12	49	10	2	0	12	4.027
11	4	446	0	2	31	35	3	2	1	4.616
12	5	534	1	23	34	14	1	0	15	4.877
13	3	198	0	8	45	20	0	0	8	3.164
14	4	463	0	3	40	29	1	0	2	4.384
15	4	431	0	6	52	15	0	0	10	4.123
16	3	209	0	2	43	27	1	0	3	3.370
17	4	401	0	7	41	23	1	1	7	4.288
18	4	440	0	8	48	16	1	0	9	4.137
IN	**35**	**3,584**	**1**	**71**	**383**	**189**	**10**	**3**		**36.986**
TOTAL	**71**	**7,270**	**6**	**195**	**779**	**304**	**24**	**6**		**73.233**

CHAMPIONSHIP HOLE SUMMARY

HOLE	PAR	YARDS	EAGLES	BIRDIES	PARS	BOGEYS	D.BOGEYS	OTHER	RANK	AVERAGE
1	4	421	0	41	316	80	16	5	6	4.190
2	5	574	7	179	235	30	6	1	17	4.677
3	3	177	0	71	329	57	1	0	14	2.974
4	4	482	0	40	304	98	15	1	5	4.201
5	4	374	4	111	297	33	8	5	15	3.882
6	3	194	0	48	330	74	5	1	10	3.085
7	5	592	11	128	242	70	6	1	16	4.871
8	4	434	1	61	297	87	11	1	9	4.107
9	4	432	0	43	303	103	8	1	7	4.172
OUT	36	3,680	23	722	2,653	632	76	16		36.159
10	4	447	0	81	311	59	7	0	13	3.983
11	4	474	0	41	249	141	21	6	1	4.352
12	5	532	8	188	216	42	4	0	18	4.664
13	3	194	1	65	324	64	4	0	12	3.011
14	4	473	0	34	255	150	14	5	2	4.349
15	4	426	0	69	281	98	9	1	8	4.109
16	3	236	0	24	305	122	6	1	3	3.247
17	4	408	0	71	302	71	10	4	11	4.072
18	4	474	0	44	284	114	13	3	4	4.229
IN	35	3,664	9	617	2,527	861	88	20		36.015
TOTAL	71	7,344	32	1,339	5,180	1,493	164	36		72.175

An Irishman with golden hands

John Hopkins on what made Shane Lowry the Champion Golfer of the Year

There was always a suspicion that The 148th Open in the seaside town of Portrush at the tip of Northern Ireland was going to be special. To have suspected that an Irishman would win at this ruggedly magnificent setting, perhaps the most impressive of all the courses on The Open pool, amidst many warm and hospitable people who were delighted at getting a major sporting event back to this once war-torn country, seemed so appropriate.

On the eve of The Open it was not wishful thinking that the winner would be Rory McIlroy, who had grown up nearby and who has represented the country of his birth with charm and success these past few years. How appropriate that would be with The Open returning to this part of the world after nearly 70 years.

What we might not have expected was that Shane Lowry would be the winner because Lowry, 32, had missed the halfway cut at the previous four Opens and had lost his playing rights in the US at the end of 2018. If it can be said that a 6ft 1in Irishman weighing more than 15 stone can come in under the radar at an event in Ireland, then Lowry did.

Never doubt that Lowry is as Irish as whiskey. He has the Irish flag on his golf shoes and paints a shamrock on his golf balls. Given the choice of attending his grandmother's 80th birthday or the wedding of McIlroy, he chose the former. "I'm Irish," he said. "Family's important."

Lowry has a measured tread that doesn't look as though it could be hurried, a build that suggests he won't easily be blown over and the nature of a

A hug from runner-up Tommy Fleetwood.

man who would be quite happy drinking from the Claret Jug for a long time. Indeed, his post-victory celebrations may have set a record for longevity.

Lowry comes from County Offaly in the middle of Ireland, four hours south of Portrush, and his family are steeped in Gaelic football as others are steeped in golf or cricket or horse racing. And thereby hangs a tale.

It seems that there was no knowledge of golf in the family when Shane set out for his first game with his cousin, so it was only natural that his mother would do as she always did and put the appropriate footwear by the door for him to pick up on his way out. Trouble was, they were Shane's Gaelic football boots, not golf shoes.

Some years ago Pete Cowen had concluded a coaching session with the promising youngsters of Ireland when an official of the Golfing Union of Ireland said to him: "I suspect there's only one of that lot with real talent." He was referring to McIlroy. On the contrary, Cowen replied: "There's another. The fat kid with glasses."

When Lowry won the Portugal Masters in 2012, his first victory as a professional although he had won the 2009 Irish Open as an amateur, he sent a message to Cowen. It read: "Not bad for a fat kid with glasses."

As well as an ability to play golf at the very highest level, Champion golfers have gifts that are as much a part of them as their own DNA. Lowry's secret lies in his hands. He has a God-given talent that enables him to play the most deft strokes with as much ease as he crashes a drive. To some golfers, the hands are hammer mitts; to Lowry they are golden. He makes difficult shots around a green seem as easy as putting the key to his house into its lock in broad daylight.

"I loved playing practice rounds with Shane," said Portrush's own Graeme McDowell. "He'd throw a few balls down around the green and let them roll behind a hump or down in a dip and from there he'd get the ball so close to the hole that I'd be scratching my head. I'd say to him: 'How did you do you do that?' And he'd look at me, puzzled. 'Haven't a clue,' he'd say. 'I just did it.'"

Does any country of comparable size produce golfers with such regularity and competence? With five victories in the past 13 Opens by Padraig Harrington (2007, 2008), Darren Clarke (2011), Rory McIlroy (2014) and now Lowry, men from the island of Ireland have had considerable success in this major championship. This does not include the US Open wins of McDowell in 2010 and McIlroy in 2011 and the PGA Championships of Harrington in 2008 and McIlroy in 2012 and 2014. Ireland is indeed a vivid green seam in the fabric of golf.

Shane Lowry, Champion Golfer of the Year. Has a ring to it, doesn't it? It is no more than he deserves — and no more than the country he comes from deserves.

A tear or two at the presentation of the Claret Jug.

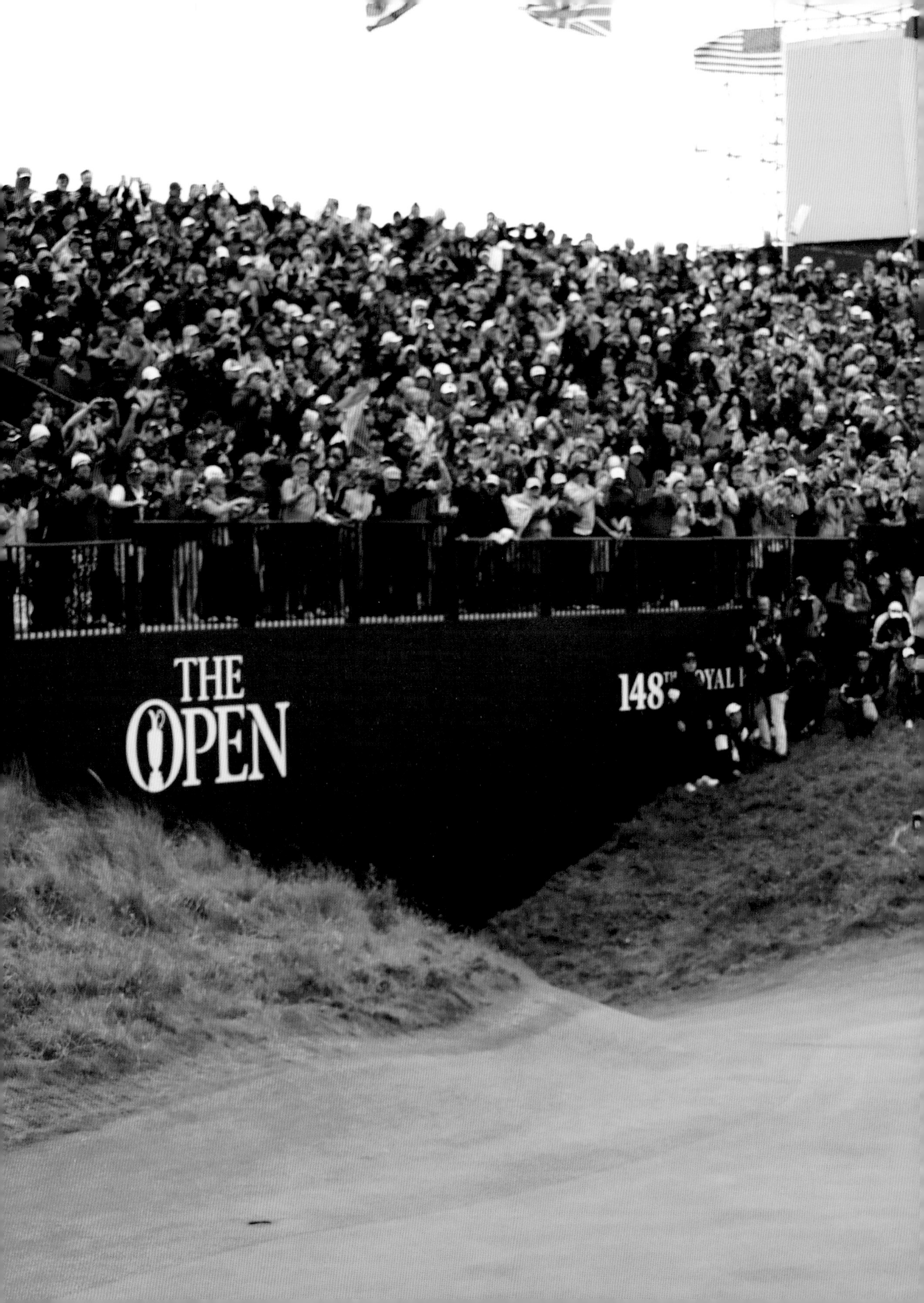
THE
OPEN

Complete Scores

Royal Portrush, Portrush, Northern Ireland 18-21 July 2019

HOLE			1	2	3	4	5	6	7	8	9	10	11	12	13	14	15	16	17	18		
PAR	POS		4	5	3	4	4	3	5	4	4	4	5	3	4	4	3	4	4		TOTAL	
Shane Lowry	2	Rd 1	4	5	2	4	3	3	5	4	3	3	5	4	3	4	4	3	4	4	67		
Republic of Ireland	T1	Rd 2	3	4	2	4	3	3	5	3	4	3	4	5	3	5	4	3	4	5	67		
$1,935,000	1	Rd 3	4	5	2	4	3	3	5	4	3	3	4	4	3	4	3	2	3	4	63		
	1	Rd 4	5	5	3	3	3	3	4	5	5	4	5	5	3	5	3	3	4	4	72	-15	**269**
Tommy Fleetwood	T3	Rd 1	4	5	2	4	4	3	4	4	4	4	4	5	2	4	4	3	4	4	68		
England	T3	Rd 2	5	4	3	4	3	3	5	4	4	4	4	4	2	4	3	4	4	3	67		
$1,120,000	2	Rd 3	3	5	3	4	3	3	4	4	3	4	4	3	4	4	3	4	4	4	66		
	2	Rd 4	4	5	4	4	3	3	5	5	4	5	4	4	3	6	4	3	4	4	74	-9	**275**
Tony Finau	T3	Rd 1	4	5	3	3	4	3	5	4	4	3	4	4	3	4	4	3	4	4	68		
USA	T12	Rd 2	5	5	3	4	4	3	4	3	4	3	4	4	4	4	3	4	4	5	70		
$718,000	T8	Rd 3	4	4	3	4	3	3	5	4	3	4	5	5	3	4	4	3	4	3	68		
	3	Rd 4	4	5	3	4	4	3	4	4	4	4	5	4	4	4	3	4	4	4	71	-7	**277**
Lee Westwood	T3	Rd 1	4	5	3	5	3	2	4	4	4	4	5	4	3	5	4	2	4	3	68		
England	T3	Rd 2	4	5	3	4	4	3	5	4	4	4	4	4	2	4	4	2	3	4	67		
$503,500	T6	Rd 3	4	4	2	3	4	3	5	4	4	5	4	5	3	4	5	3	4	4	70		
	T4	Rd 4	5	4	2	4	3	3	5	4	5	3	5	6	4	4	4	4	4	4	73	-6	**278**
Brooks Koepka	T3	Rd 1	4	4	3	4	3	3	5	4	4	4	4	3	3	4	3	5	4	4	68		
USA	T8	Rd 2	4	4	3	5	4	3	5	4	4	4	4	4	2	4	4	3	4	4	69		
$503,500	T4	Rd 3	4	4	3	4	4	4	4	4	4	4	4	4	3	5	3	3	3	3	67		
	T4	Rd 4	5	6	4	5	2	3	5	4	4	4	5	5	3	4	3	3	5	4	74	-6	**278**
Robert MacIntyre	T3	Rd 1	3	4	3	5	2	3	4	4	5	4	4	4	3	5	4	3	3	5	68		
Scotland	T25	Rd 2	4	5	3	5	4	3	5	3	4	3	4	5	3	5	5	2	4	5	72		
$313,000	T29	Rd 3	4	4	3	4	4	3	5	4	4	4	5	5	3	4	5	3	3	4	71		
	T6	Rd 4	4	4	3	4	4	3	4	4	4	3	4	5	3	5	4	3	4	3	68	-5	**279**
Tyrrell Hatton	T3	Rd 1	4	5	3	4	3	3	5	4	4	4	4	3	3	4	3	3	3	5	68		
England	T18	Rd 2	4	5	4	3	4	3	2	4	4	4	4	4	3	5	4	5	4	4	71		
$313,000	T23	Rd 3	4	4	3	5	3	3	5	4	4	3	3	5	4	4	4	4	4	5	71		
	T6	Rd 4	4	4	3	3	4	3	6	4	4	4	4	4	3	5	4	3	3	4	69	-5	**279**
Danny Willett	T94	Rd 1	4	4	4	4	4	3	5	3	3	3	6	6	3	6	4	3	5	4	74		
England	T32	Rd 2	4	4	3	4	3	3	5	4	4	4	4	4	4	4	3	3	4	3	67		
$313,000	T8	Rd 3	4	5	2	4	3	3	5	3	4	3	4	4	3	4	4	3	3	4	65		
	T6	Rd 4	4	4	3	4	4	3	4	4	5	4	5	4	4	5	5	3	4	4	73	-5	**279**

(a) Denotes amateur

HOLE		1	2	3	4	5	6	7	8	9	10	11	12	13	14	15	16	17	18			
PAR	POS	4	5	3	4	4	3	5	4	4	4	5	3	4	4	3	4	3	4	TOTAL		
Rickie Fowler	T20 Rd 1	4	5	3	4	3	4	4	4	5	4	3	5	3	4	4	3	5	3	70		
USA	T18 Rd 2	5	5	3	4	4	2	5	4	4	4	4	4	2	5	3	3	4	4	69		
$313,000	T6 Rd 3	4	5	3	5	3	3	4	4	4	3	3	5	3	4	3	3	3	4	66		
	T6 Rd 4	6	4	2	3	4	3	5	4	4	6	4	5	4	5	3	3	5	4	74	-5	**279**
Patrick Reed	T42 Rd 1	4	5	3	3	4	3	6	4	4	4	5	4	4	4	4	3	3	4	71		
USA	T12 Rd 2	4	5	2	3	4	2	4	4	4	4	5	5	2	4	4	3	4	4	67		
$223,000	T19 Rd 3	4	5	3	4	4	4	4	4	4	4	4	4	4	4	4	3	4	4	71		
	10 Rd 4	4	5	2	4	5	3	4	4	5	4	4	4	3	4	4	3	5	4	71	-4	**280**
Francesco Molinari	T94 Rd 1	4	4	3	4	4	4	5	6	4	4	5	6	3	3	4	3	4	4	74		
Italy	T58 Rd 2	4	5	3	4	4	3	4	3	4	4	3	5	3	4	4	3	5	4	69		
$171,700	T54 Rd 3	4	5	3	4	3	3	5	5	4	4	5	5	3	3	4	3	4	4	72		
	T11 Rd 4	4	4	3	4	4	3	4	4	4	4	4	3	3	4	4	3	3	4	66	-3	**281**
Tom Lewis	T113 Rd 1	5	7	3	4	3	3	5	5	4	4	5	4	2	5	3	3	6	4	75		
England	T58 Rd 2	5	5	3	4	4	3	4	4	4	3	3	4	3	4	4	3	4	4	68		
$171,700	T29 Rd 3	4	3	4	4	4	4	5	4	3	4	4	4	3	3	4	3	4	4	68		
	T11 Rd 4	4	5	3	3	3	3	4	5	4	4	5	5	3	4	4	3	4	4	70	-3	**281**
Justin Thomas	T42 Rd 1	5	5	3	6	3	3	5	4	3	3	4	5	3	3	4	3	4	5	71		
USA	T32 Rd 2	5	5	3	5	4	3	5	4	4	5	4	4	2	4	3	3	4	3	70		
$171,700	T19 Rd 3	4	4	3	4	3	3	5	3	4	4	4	3	4	5	4	3	4	4	68		
	T11 Rd 4	4	5	2	3	3	3	4	4	5	4	4	6	2	5	4	3	7	4	72	-3	**281**
Alex Noren	T3 Rd 1	3	5	3	3	4	3	5	3	5	4	3	4	3	5	4	3	4	4	68		
Sweden	T18 Rd 2	4	5	3	4	3	2	5	4	5	4	4	4	3	5	5	2	4	5	71		
$171,700	T12 Rd 3	4	4	3	3	4	3	5	4	5	4	3	6	2	4	4	3	3	4	68		
	T11 Rd 4	4	5	3	5	4	3	5	4	3	4	5	5	3	5	4	4	4	4	74	-3	**281**
Jon Rahm	T3 Rd 1	4	4	3	3	4	3	4	3	4	3	4	5	3	4	5	3	4	5	68		
Spain	T12 Rd 2	4	7	2	4	4	3	5	4	3	4	4	4	3	4	4	3	4	4	70		
$171,700	T8 Rd 3	4	4	3	4	4	4	5	3	4	4	4	5	3	3	4	2	3	5	68		
	T11 Rd 4	6	5	4	4	5	3	5	3	4	4	5	4	4	4	4	3	5	3	75	-3	**281**
Ryan Fox	T3 Rd 1	5	5	4	4	4	3	5	4	5	4	4	2	3	3	3	3	3	3	68		
New Zealand	T58 Rd 2	5	5	4	4	3	3	5	4	4	4	5	5	3	6	3	3	4	5	75		
$126,313	T43 Rd 3	4	4	3	4	3	4	5	3	4	3	4	5	4	5	4	3	5	3	70		
	T16 Rd 4	4	5	3	4	4	3	5	3	4	4	3	4	4	4	4	4	3	4	69	-2	**282**
Lucas Bjerregaard	T20 Rd 1	4	5	3	6	4	3	5	4	4	5	4	3	3	3	3	3	3	4	70		
Denmark	T12 Rd 2	4	4	3	4	4	3	4	3	4	4	3	4	4	4	5	3	4	4	68		
$126,313	T36 Rd 3	4	5	2	6	4	2	6	4	4	4	5	5	3	5	5	3	3	4	74		
	T16 Rd 4	5	5	3	4	3	3	4	4	4	3	4	5	4	4	4	3	5	3	70	-2	**282**
Rory Sabbatini	T20 Rd 1	4	4	4	4	4	3	5	5	4	3	3	5	3	4	4	4	4	4	70		
Slovakia	T25 Rd 2	4	5	3	4	4	3	5	4	4	4	4	3	4	3	4	4	4	4	70		
$126,313	T29 Rd 3	4	5	3	5	5	3	5	3	4	3	5	4	3	4	4	3	4	4	71		
	T16 Rd 4	4	5	3	4	4	3	5	4	5	4	5	4	2	5	4	3	3	4	71	-2	**282**
Sang Hyun Park	T16 Rd 1	4	4	3	4	3	4	5	4	4	3	4	3	4	4	3	4	4	4	69		
Korea	T32 Rd 2	4	6	3	4	3	3	3	4	5	3	4	5	3	6	4	3	4	5	72		
$126,313	T19 Rd 3	4	4	3	3	3	3	5	4	4	3	4	5	3	3	5	4	4	4	68		
	T16 Rd 4	4	6	3	4	4	3	5	3	4	4	4	5	3	5	4	3	4	5	73	-2	**282**
Louis Oosthuizen	T20 Rd 1	4	4	3	4	4	3	6	4	4	3	5	4	2	4	3	4	4	5	70		
South Africa	T48 Rd 2	4	5	3	4	3	2	5	5	4	4	5	3	5	4	4	4	5	3	72		
$91,350	T50 Rd 3	4	5	3	5	4	3	5	4	3	4	4	4	3	5	4	4	4	4	72		
	T20 Rd 4	4	4	3	4	3	3	5	5	3	3	4	6	3	4	4	3	5	3	69	-1	**283**

HOLE			1	2	3	4	5	6	7	8	9	10	11	12	13	14	15	16	17	18			
PAR	POS		4	5	3	4	4	3	5	4	4	4	4	5	3	4	4	3	4	4		**TOTAL**	
Stewart Cink	T94	Rd 1	4	5	4	5	3	3	5	4	4	4	5	5	3	4	4	4	4	4	74		
USA	T48	Rd 2	4	4	3	5	3	2	6	4	4	4	4	4	2	4	4	3	3	5	68		
$91,350	T43	Rd 3	4	4	3	4	3	4	6	4	4	4	5	5	3	4	4	4	3	4	71		
	T20	Rd 4	4	4	3	4	3	3	4	4	5	5	4	5	3	4	4	3	4	4	70	-1	**283**
Doc Redman	T42	Rd 1	6	5	4	3	4	3	4	4	4	3	4	5	3	4	4	3	4	4	71		
USA	T48	Rd 2	3	6	3	4	4	2	5	4	3	5	4	5	2	4	5	3	4	5	71		
$91,350	T43	Rd 3	4	4	2	3	4	3	5	5	4	4	5	5	3	4	3	3	5	5	71		
	T20	Rd 4	5	4	2	4	3	3	4	4	4	3	5	6	3	4	5	3	4	4	70	-1	**283**
Lucas Glover	T54	Rd 1	4	4	4	4	4	3	5	5	4	4	3	5	3	4	4	3	4	5	72		
USA	T32	Rd 2	3	4	3	4	4	3	5	4	4	3	4	4	3	5	4	3	4	5	69		
$91,350	T36	Rd 3	4	4	2	3	4	4	5	5	4	3	4	5	3	3	5	3	5	5	71		
	T20	Rd 4	5	4	4	4	3	2	5	4	4	4	4	4	3	4	4	3	5	5	71	-1	**283**
Erik van Rooyen	T20	Rd 1	4	5	3	5	3	3	5	4	3	4	3	5	3	3	5	3	4	5	70		
South Africa	T12	Rd 2	4	5	2	4	3	3	4	4	4	4	4	5	3	4	4	3	4	4	68		
$91,350	T23	Rd 3	4	6	3	4	5	3	5	4	3	4	5	5	3	5	4	3	3	4	72		
	T20	Rd 4	4	4	3	4	4	4	5	4	3	4	5	5	3	5	4	3	4	5	73	-1	**283**
Matthew Fitzpatrick	T42	Rd 1	4	5	4	4	4	3	4	3	4	4	4	4	3	5	5	3	4	4	71		
England	T25	Rd 2	4	4	3	3	4	3	4	4	4	4	4	4	3	6	4	3	4	4	69		
$91,350	T23	Rd 3	5	4	3	4	4	3	4	4	4	5	4	4	3	4	4	3	4	4	70		
	T20	Rd 4	6	5	2	4	4	2	5	4	4	4	5	4	3	4	5	3	5	4	73	-1	**283**
Cameron Smith	T20	Rd 1	5	4	3	4	4	3	5	4	4	3	4	5	3	4	4	3	4	4	70		
Australia	T5	Rd 2	4	4	3	4	4	3	4	3	5	3	4	4	2	4	4	3	4	4	66		
$91,350	T12	Rd 3	4	4	4	4	4	3	5	4	4	5	4	3	2	6	4	3	4	4	71		
	T20	Rd 4	4	5	3	5	3	4	5	5	4	3	5	5	3	4	5	4	5	4	76	-1	**283**
Henrik Stenson	T20	Rd 1	4	4	3	4	4	3	6	3	4	4	5	4	3	4	4	3	4	4	70		
Sweden	T18	Rd 2	4	5	2	4	4	3	4	5	4	3	4	4	3	5	4	3	4	4	69		
$91,350	T12	Rd 3	4	4	2	4	4	3	5	3	4	4	4	5	3	5	4	3	4	3	68		
	T20	Rd 4	5	5	3	5	4	4	4	4	5	3	4	5	2	5	4	4	5	5	76	-1	**283**
Jordan Spieth	T20	Rd 1	4	4	2	4	3	3	5	6	4	4	5	4	3	4	4	3	4	4	70		
USA	T8	Rd 2	4	5	3	4	3	2	3	3	5	4	4	4	3	5	4	3	4	4	67		
$91,350	T8	Rd 3	4	4	2	4	4	4	5	4	5	4	5	4	3	4	3	3	3	4	69		
	T20	Rd 4	4	4	4	5	4	3	6	4	4	5	4	5	3	5	4	4	5	4	77	-1	**283**
Justin Rose	T16	Rd 1	3	5	3	5	4	3	5	4	4	4	4	4	3	4	4	2	4	4	69		
England	T5	Rd 2	4	4	3	5	4	3	4	4	4	3	4	4	3	3	4	3	4	4	67		
$91,350	T4	Rd 3	4	4	3	4	4	3	5	5	4	4	4	3	2	4	3	4	4	4	68		
	T20	Rd 4	4	5	4	4	4	4	5	5	6	4	5	4	4	4	5	3	5	4	79	-1	**283**
Kevin Kisner	T20	Rd 1	4	3	3	3	4	3	5	3	6	4	4	6	3	4	5	2	3	5	70		
USA	T32	Rd 2	4	6	3	5	4	3	3	4	3	4	4	4	4	5	4	3	4	4	71		
$69,875	T29	Rd 3	3	4	3	5	4	3	5	3	4	4	6	4	3	4	5	3	3	4	70		
	T30	Rd 4	4	5	3	4	5	3	4	4	4	4	5	5	3	4	4	4	4	4	73	E	**284**
Webb Simpson	T3	Rd 1	4	5	3	4	4	3	4	3	4	3	3	5	2	4	4	3	5	5	68		
USA	T18	Rd 2	4	6	3	4	3	3	4	5	4	4	4	5	3	4	3	3	4	5	71		
$69,875	T23	Rd 3	4	4	2	4	4	3	6	4	4	4	4	5	3	4	4	3	5	4	71		
	T30	Rd 4	4	5	3	4	3	3	5	4	5	4	5	5	3	4	5	4	3	5	74	E	**284**
Kiradech Aphibarnrat	T3	Rd 1	4	4	3	4	4	3	5	4	4	4	4	4	3	4	4	3	4	3	68		
Thailand	T32	Rd 2	3	5	3	5	3	3	7	4	3	4	4	5	3	4	5	4	4	4	73		
$56,278	T68	Rd 3	5	5	3	6	4	3	4	5	4	4	5	5	4	5	4	3	4	5	77		
	T32	Rd 4	5	3	2	4	3	3	5	5	4	4	4	4	3	4	5	2	4	3	67	+1	**285**

HOLE		1	2	3	4	5	6	7	8	9	10	11	12	13	14	15	16	17	18	
PAR POS		4	5	3	4	4	3	5	4	4	4	4	5	3	4	4	3	4	4	TOTAL
Jason Kokrak T94	Rd 1	4	4	3	4	4	3	6	4	5	5	4	5	3	4	4	3	4	5	74
USA T58	Rd 2	4	4	4	4	4	3	3	6	4	4	4	4	3	4	4	3	4	3	69
$56,278 T66	Rd 3	4	5	3	4	4	3	5	4	4	4	5	5	3	5	4	4	4	4	74
T32	Rd 4	4	5	2	4	3	2	4	5	4	4	4	4	4	5	4	2	4	4	68 +1 **285**
Bernd Wiesberger T20	Rd 1	4	5	2	4	4	3	5	5	4	4	4	5	2	4	4	3	4	4	70
Austria T32	Rd 2	5	5	3	5	4	3	4	4	4	4	4	5	2	5	4	3	3	4	71
$56,278 T54	Rd 3	5	5	3	4	4	4	5	5	4	4	4	5	4	4	3	3	3	5	74
T32	Rd 4	4	5	3	4	4	3	4	4	4	4	4	5	3	4	4	3	4	4	70 +1 **285**
Andrew Wilson T128	Rd 1	4	5	3	4	4	3	4	4	3	4	5	6	3	5	5	4	5	5	76
England T58	Rd 2	3	5	2	4	4	2	5	4	3	4	3	4	4	5	4	3	4	4	67
$56,278 T50	Rd 3	4	4	4	5	4	3	4	4	4	4	5	5	4	4	3	3	3	4	71
T32	Rd 4	5	5	4	4	3	3	4	4	4	6	4	4	3	4	4	3	4	3	71 +1 **285**
Joost Luiten T72	Rd 1	4	5	4	5	4	3	5	3	4	4	4	4	3	4	3	3	7	4	73
Netherlands T48	Rd 2	4	5	3	4	4	4	4	4	4	4	3	5	3	4	3	4	3	4	69
$56,278 T43	Rd 3	4	4	3	4	3	3	5	4	5	5	3	4	2	4	4	4	5	5	71
T32	Rd 4	4	4	2	4	3	3	5	4	5	4	5	4	4	4	3	3	5	5	72 +1 **285**
Ernie Els T42	Rd 1	4	5	2	6	4	2	5	4	4	4	4	6	3	3	4	3	4	4	71
South Africa T25	Rd 2	4	5	3	4	4	3	4	3	4	4	4	4	4	4	3	4	4	69
$56,278 T36	Rd 3	4	4	2	5	4	4	6	3	4	4	5	4	4	4	3	4	4	72
T32	Rd 4	4	5	3	4	4	3	4	4	5	4	5	3	4	5	3	5	4	73 +1 **285**
Byeong Hun An T72	Rd 1	3	4	3	4	4	3	6	4	4	6	4	5	3	5	3	3	4	5	73
Korea T25	Rd 2	4	4	3	4	3	4	4	4	4	4	4	3	4	3	4	4	4	67
$56,278 T23	Rd 3	4	4	3	3	3	3	5	3	5	5	4	3	4	4	4	4	5	70
T32	Rd 4	4	5	4	4	4	3	5	4	4	4	5	4	4	4	4	4	5	75 +1 **285**
Andrew Putnam T20	Rd 1	4	5	4	4	4	3	4	4	4	4	5	4	3	3	4	3	4	4	70
USA T8	Rd 2	3	5	3	4	4	3	5	4	4	3	4	3	3	4	4	3	4	4	67
$56,278 T12	Rd 3	4	6	3	4	3	3	5	4	4	4	4	2	4	5	3	4	4	70
T32	Rd 4	6	5	3	4	3	4	5	5	5	4	4	5	3	5	5	4	4	4	78 +1 **285**
Dylan Frittelli T3	Rd 1	4	5	3	4	4	3	5	3	4	4	3	4	3	4	3	3	4	5	68
South Africa T8	Rd 2	4	4	3	4	4	3	5	4	4	3	3	4	3	4	3	3	6	5	69
$56,278 T12	Rd 3	4	4	3	6	4	3	3	4	4	4	3	5	3	4	4	3	4	5	70
T32	Rd 4	4	5	4	4	3	3	5	5	5	4	5	4	4	5	4	4	5	5	78 +1 **285**
Callum Shinkwin T20	Rd 1	4	4	3	4	4	3	5	4	5	3	5	3	4	3	3	4	5	70
England T32	Rd 2	4	5	3	4	4	3	5	6	4	4	5	3	2	4	4	3	4	4	71
$36,925 T61	Rd 3	4	5	4	4	3	3	4	4	4	6	6	3	5	4	3	5	4	75
T41	Rd 4	4	4	3	4	5	3	4	4	5	4	4	4	3	4	4	3	4	4	70 +2 **286**
Kyle Stanley T113	Rd 1	4	4	3	4	4	5	6	4	4	4	5	5	3	4	4	4	4	4	75
USA T48	Rd 2	4	4	2	5	4	2	3	4	4	4	5	5	3	4	4	2	4	4	67
$36,925 T54	Rd 3	3	4	3	4	6	3	5	3	4	5	4	4	4	5	5	3	4	4	73
T41	Rd 4	4	4	3	4	4	3	5	4	4	4	6	4	3	4	4	3	4	4	71 +2 **286**
Benjamin Hebert T72	Rd 1	5	4	2	5	4	4	5	4	4	4	4	5	3	4	5	3	4	4	73
France T48	Rd 2	4	5	3	4	4	3	4	4	5	4	4	4	2	4	5	3	3	4	69
$36,925 T54	Rd 3	4	4	3	4	4	4	6	3	4	4	4	5	2	5	4	4	5	4	73
T41	Rd 4	3	5	4	4	4	3	4	4	4	4	5	5	3	4	4	3	4	4	71 +2 **286**
Innchoon Hwang T54	Rd 1	4	5	3	4	4	4	5	5	4	3	4	6	3	3	3	4	4	4	72
Korea T58	Rd 2	3	6	3	4	4	2	5	5	4	4	4	5	3	4	3	3	4	5	71
$36,925 T43	Rd 3	4	5	3	3	3	5	4	5	4	3	5	5	3	3	4	4	4	3	70
T41	Rd 4	3	4	3	5	3	4	4	5	4	3	5	6	4	4	4	4	4	4	73 +2 **286**

HOLE			1	2	3	4	5	6	7	8	9	10	11	12	13	14	15	16	17	18		
PAR	POS		4	5	3	4	4	3	5	4	4	4	4	5	3	4	4	3	4	4		TOTAL
Aaron Wise	T54	Rd 1	3	5	3	4	4	3	6	4	3	4	5	4	3	5	4	3	4	5	72	
USA	T32	Rd 2	4	4	3	5	4	3	6	3	4	4	4	4	3	4	3	3	4	4	69	
$36,925	T36	Rd 3	5	3	3	5	4	3	4	3	4	4	4	4	3	4	4	4	4	6	71	
	T41	Rd 4	6	5	3	4	3	3	4	5	4	4	5	5	3	3	4	4	4	5	74	+2 **286**
Patrick Cantlay	T20	Rd 1	4	4	3	4	3	4	6	4	4	4	4	5	3	4	3	2	4	5	70	
USA	T32	Rd 2	4	5	3	4	4	3	5	5	4	4	4	5	3	4	3	3	4	4	71	
$36,925	T36	Rd 3	4	4	2	4	5	3	4	5	4	4	5	4	3	4	5	3	4	4	71	
	T41	Rd 4	4	5	3	4	4	3	5	4	4	4	5	5	3	5	4	3	5	4	74	+2 **286**
Justin Harding	T42	Rd 1	5	4	2	4	6	3	4	3	4	4	5	4	3	4	5	4	3	4	71	
South Africa	T5	Rd 2	4	4	3	5	4	3	3	4	4	3	4	4	2	5	3	2	4	4	65	
$36,925	T23	Rd 3	4	5	2	3	6	4	5	3	3	4	5	6	3	4	6	3	4	4	74	
	T41	Rd 4	4	5	2	4	4	4	5	7	4	4	4	4	4	4	5	3	4	5	76	+2 **286**
Russell Knox	T20	Rd 1	4	4	3	3	4	3	6	4	4	4	4	4	3	5	4	3	4	4	70	
Scotland	T32	Rd 2	4	5	3	4	3	3	6	4	4	5	3	4	3	5	4	3	4	4	71	
$36,925	T19	Rd 3	4	4	3	4	4	3	5	4	3	4	4	4	3	5	5	3	3	3	68	
	T41	Rd 4	4	5	4	4	3	3	4	5	5	5	5	6	3	5	5	3	4	4	77	+2 **286**
Xander Schauffele	T94	Rd 1	3	4	3	4	3	4	5	4	5	4	6	5	3	4	4	4	4	5	74	
USA	T18	Rd 2	4	5	3	4	4	3	4	3	4	4	4	3	3	4	3	3	3	4	65	
$36,925	18	Rd 3	4	4	3	4	4	3	4	3	4	3	4	5	3	5	4	4	4	4	69	
	T41	Rd 4	4	5	3	5	3	3	5	6	4	4	5	6	4	4	4	4	5	4	78	+2 **286**
Matt Kuchar	T20	Rd 1	4	4	3	4	3	4	6	4	3	5	4	4	3	4	4	3	4	4	70	
USA	T12	Rd 2	5	4	2	5	4	2	5	4	4	3	4	4	3	4	4	3	4	4	68	
$36,925	T12	Rd 3	4	4	3	4	4	3	5	4	3	4	4	5	3	4	4	3	4	4	69	
	T41	Rd 4	4	5	3	5	6	2	5	4	5	4	5	5	3	4	5	5	5	4	79	+2 **286**
Shubhankar Sharma	T20	Rd 1	4	5	3	4	4	3	5	4	4	4	4	5	2	4	4	3	4	4	70	
India	T48	Rd 2	5	4	3	5	4	2	4	4	4	4	4	6	3	5	4	3	4	4	72	
$28,317	72	Rd 3	4	4	3	4	6	3	5	4	3	6	6	4	4	5	6	3	4	3	77	
	T51	Rd 4	5	4	2	4	4	3	5	3	4	4	4	5	2	5	3	4	4	3	68	+3 **287**
Branden Grace	T20	Rd 1	4	5	3	4	3	3	5	4	5	3	5	4	2	5	4	3	4	4	70	
South Africa	T32	Rd 2	4	6	2	4	4	3	5	4	4	3	4	5	2	5	4	4	4	4	71	
$28,317	T61	Rd 3	4	5	3	4	4	3	6	4	4	4	5	4	4	5	4	3	4	5	75	
	T51	Rd 4	4	4	3	5	3	3	4	5	4	3	5	5	3	4	4	4	4	4	71	+3 **287**
Bubba Watson	T54	Rd 1	4	5	3	4	4	3	6	4	4	5	4	4	2	4	3	4	4	5	72	
USA	T58	Rd 2	4	5	3	4	4	2	4	4	5	4	5	4	3	4	5	3	4	4	71	
$28,317	T61	Rd 3	4	5	4	4	3	3	5	5	4	5	4	4	3	4	4	4	4	4	73	
	T51	Rd 4	4	3	3	5	3	3	6	4	5	4	5	4	3	5	4	3	3	4	71	+3 **287**
Matthew Wallace	T72	Rd 1	4	5	3	6	4	5	5	3	4	3	4	4	3	4	6	3	3	4	73	
England	T58	Rd 2	4	5	4	3	4	3	5	4	4	4	4	4	3	3	5	4	3	4	70	
$28,317	T54	Rd 3	5	4	4	4	4	3	5	4	4	4	5	5	2	5	5	3	3	4	72	
	T51	Rd 4	4	5	3	3	4	3	4	4	4	5	4	5	4	5	4	3	4	4	72	+3 **287**
Charley Hoffman	T20	Rd 1	4	5	3	4	3	3	5	4	4	4	5	2	4	3	4	5	4	70		
USA	T58	Rd 2	4	5	3	4	4	3	5	5	4	4	5	4	3	4	5	3	4	4	73	
$28,317	T43	Rd 3	4	4	3	4	4	4	6	3	4	4	5	4	3	4	3	3	3	4	70	
	T51	Rd 4	5	5	3	4	4	3	4	5	4	4	5	6	3	4	4	3	4	4	74	+3 **287**
Dustin Johnson	T54	Rd 1	4	5	3	5	4	2	5	5	3	4	4	5	2	4	5	3	4	5	72	
USA	T18	Rd 2	4	4	3	3	4	2	5	4	4	4	5	4	3	5	4	2	4	3	67	
$28,317	T29	Rd 3	4	4	3	5	4	3	6	4	4	4	4	5	2	5	3	3	4	5	72	
	T51	Rd 4	4	4	3	5	3	3	6	5	5	4	4	5	3	5	4	4	4	5	76	+3 **287**

HOLE			1	2	3	4	5	6	7	8	9	10	11	12	13	14	15	16	17	18		
PAR	POS		4	5	3	4	4	3	5	4	4	4	4	5	3	4	4	3	4	4		TOTAL
Ashton Turner	T16	Rd 1	4	4	4	4	3	3	5	4	4	4	3	5	2	4	4	3	4	5	69	
England	T58	Rd 2	5	5	3	5	4	2	6	4	4	4	5	4	3	4	4	3	4	5	74	
$26,467	73	Rd 3	5	5	3	5	4	3	5	5	4	4	5	5	3	5	5	4	3	4	77	
	T57	Rd 4	4	5	3	4	2	3	6	4	4	3	6	4	2	4	4	3	4	3	68	+4 **288**
Thorbjørn Olesen	T54	Rd 1	4	4	3	4	4	3	5	4	4	4	3	3	5	4	4	4	4	4	72	
Denmark	T25	Rd 2	4	5	3	4	4	4	4	4	4	4	3	4	3	4	4	2	4	4	68	
$26,467	T66	Rd 3	4	4	4	3	5	3	6	4	5	4	7	5	3	4	5	3	4	4	77	
	T57	Rd 4	4	4	3	5	4	3	4	5	5	4	3	4	4	4	4	3	4	4	71	+4 **288**
Kevin Streelman	T140	Rd 1	4	6	3	4	4	4	5	5	5	4	5	4	2	3	7	4	4	4	77	
USA	T48	Rd 2	3	4	3	3	4	3	4	5	3	4	4	4	3	3	4	3	4	4	65	
$26,467	T61	Rd 3	4	4	4	5	4	3	4	6	4	5	4	5	3	4	4	4	3	4	74	
	T57	Rd 4	4	5	3	4	5	3	4	4	5	5	5	5	4	3	3	3	5	4	72	+4 **288**
Paul Casey	T54	Rd 1	4	5	4	4	3	3	5	4	3	4	4	6	3	4	5	3	4	4	72	
England	T48	Rd 2	4	4	3	5	4	3	5	4	4	4	4	5	2	5	3	3	4	4	70	
$26,467	T54	Rd 3	4	4	3	4	4	3	6	5	5	4	4	4	3	4	4	3	4	5	73	
	T57	Rd 4	4	4	3	4	3	3	5	4	4	4	4	5	3	4	5	4	5	5	73	+4 **288**
Adam Hadwin	T94	Rd 1	4	5	3	4	5	3	6	3	5	4	4	5	3	4	5	3	4	4	74	
Canada	T58	Rd 2	4	4	3	4	4	3	4	2	4	4	4	6	3	4	4	4	4	4	69	
$26,467	T54	Rd 3	3	5	3	4	4	3	5	4	5	4	4	3	6	4	3	3	5	2	72	
	T57	Rd 4	3	4	3	5	4	3	3	4	5	4	6	6	4	4	4	3	4	4	73	+4 **288**
Graeme McDowell	T72	Rd 1	4	4	3	4	4	3	4	4	4	4	4	5	3	3	5	3	5	7	73	
Northern Ireland	T58	Rd 2	3	5	3	5	4	2	5	4	4	4	4	4	3	5	4	3	4	4	70	
$26,467	T29	Rd 3	4	4	3	4	4	4	5	4	4	4	3	4	3	5	4	3	3	3	68	
	T57	Rd 4	3	5	3	4	4	3	5	6	4	5	5	6	3	4	4	4	4	5	77	+4 **288**
Paul Waring	T113	Rd 1	4	4	4	4	4	4	6	4	4	4	5	4	3	5	5	3	4	4	75	
England	T58	Rd 2	4	5	3	4	3	4	4	4	4	4	4	4	4	3	3	3	4		68	
$25,800	T68	Rd 3	4	5	3	4	4	4	6	4	5	3	5	5	3	4	4	4	4	4	75	
	T63	Rd 4	3	5	3	3	3	3	7	4	5	4	4	6	2	4	4	3	4	4	71	+5 **289**
Jim Furyk	T72	Rd 1	4	4	3	4	4	3	5	4	4	5	5	5	3	4	5	4	4	3	73	
USA	T32	Rd 2	4	6	3	5	3	3	5	4	4	4	4	4	2	3	4	3	3	4	68	
$25,800	T61	Rd 3	4	5	3	4	7	3	5	4	4	4	4	4	3	5	4	4	4	4	75	
	T63	Rd 4	3	4	3	5	3	3	5	4	5	5	5	5	3	5	4	3	4	4	73	+5 **289**
Mikko Korhonen	T54	Rd 1	4	4	4	4	4	2	5	5	4	4	6	5	3	4	4	3	4	3	72	
Finland	T32	Rd 2	4	5	3	4	3	3	4	3	4	3	5	5	3	5	4	3	4	4	69	
$25,800	T36	Rd 3	5	5	2	4	4	3	4	4	5	4	5	5	3	4	3	3	4	4	71	
	T63	Rd 4	5	4	3	4	4	4	5	5	5	3	5	5	4	5	4	4	4	4	77	+5 **289**
Romain Langasque	T16	Rd 1	4	4	2	4	4	3	4	5	4	4	4	4	3	4	4	3	5	4	69	
France	T32	Rd 2	4	5	3	4	5	3	5	4	4	4	5	5	3	5	3	4	3	4	72	
$25,800	T29	Rd 3	4	4	3	4	4	3	5	4	3	4	5	4	2	5	4	3	5	4	70	
	T63	Rd 4	5	6	3	3	4	3	5	4	4	4	5	5	3	5	5	4	5	5	78	+5 **289**
Thomas Pieters	T54	Rd 1	4	5	3	5	3	3	6	4	3	4	4	4	2	4	5	3	5	5	72	
Belgium	T25	Rd 2	4	4	3	3	4	3	4	4	4	4	5	4	3	5	3	3	3	5	68	
$25,088	T50	Rd 3	4	4	2	5	4	4	5	3	4	4	4	5	3	7	4	4	4	4	74	
	T67	Rd 4	7	6	3	3	4	2	5	4	4	4	4	5	3	5	5	3	4	5	76	+6 **290**
Yosuke Asaji	T54	Rd 1	3	4	3	4	4	3	5	4	5	3	6	5	2	4	5	3	4	5	72	
Japan	T58	Rd 2	4	5	3	6	4	3	4	4	4	3	4	5	3	4	3	4	4	4	71	
$25,088	T50	Rd 3	4	4	3	4	4	3	5	4	5	4	4	3	4	4	4	4	4	4	71	
	T67	Rd 4	4	5	3	5	3	2	7	4	3	5	7	5	2	4	4	4	5	4	76	+6 **290**

HOLE			1	2	3	4	5	6	7	8	9	10	11	12	13	14	15	16	17	18		TOTAL
PAR	POS		4	5	3	4	4	3	5	4	4	4	4	5	3	4	4	3	4	4		TOTAL
Sergio Garcia	T3	Rd 1	4	5	3	4	4	3	4	3	5	4	3	4	3	4	4	3	4	4	68	
Spain	T32	Rd 2	3	5	4	5	5	3	4	4	4	4	5	5	3	4	4	4	3	4	73	
$25,088	T36	Rd 3	4	4	3	4	4	4	4	4	4	5	5	4	3	4	4	3	4	4	71	
	T67	Rd 4	4	5	3	4	6	3	6	4	4	5	5	5	3	5	4	4	4	4	78	+6 **290**
JB Holmes	1	Rd 1	5	4	2	4	3	3	5	4	4	4	4	4	3	3	4	3	4	3	66	
USA	T1	Rd 2	4	4	3	4	3	2	5	4	5	4	4	4	2	5	4	3	4	4	68	
$25,088	3	Rd 3	4	4	2	4	4	3	5	4	4	4	4	4	4	5	4	3	4	3	69	
	T67	Rd 4	6	5	3	5	4	4	4	5	5	4	7	7	3	5	4	4	6	6	87	+6 **290**
Eddie Pepperell	T20	Rd 1	4	4	3	3	4	3	5	4	5	3	5	4	2	5	4	3	5	4	70	
England	T48	Rd 2	4	5	3	4	4	3	4	5	5	4	4	4	3	5	4	4	4	3	72	
$24,625	T68	Rd 3	4	4	3	5	4	3	6	5	4	5	4	5	3	5	4	4	4	4	76	
	71	Rd 4	5	6	2	4	3	2	6	4	6	4	4	6	2	4	4	4	4	4	74	+8 **292**
Nino Bertasio	T54	Rd 1	4	5	3	4	4	3	5	4	6	4	3	5	3	4	5	2	4	4	72	
Italy	T58	Rd 2	4	6	3	4	3	3	5	3	5	4	5	4	2	5	4	3	4	4	71	
$24,438	T68	Rd 3	6	4	3	5	4	3	5	4	4	4	5	4	4	5	3	3	4	5	75	
	T72	Rd 4	5	5	3	4	4	3	5	4	5	4	4	6	4	5	4	3	4	3	75	+9 **293**
Yuki Inamori	T20	Rd 1	4	4	2	4	4	3	5	4	4	4	3	5	3	4	4	4	4	5	70	
Japan	T58	Rd 2	4	5	3	4	4	3	5	4	4	4	4	4	3	6	4	3	5	4	73	
$24,438	T43	Rd 3	5	4	3	4	4	4	5	4	3	5	3	4	4	4	3	3	4	4	70	
	T72	Rd 4	5	5	3	4	7	3	5	5	4	3	5	6	3	5	3	4	5	5	80	+9 **293**

NON QUALIFIERS AFTER 36 HOLES
(Leading 10 professionals and ties receive $7,500 each, next 20 professionals and ties receive $6,000 each, remainder of professionals receive $5,000 each.)

HOLE			1	2	3	4	5	6	7	8	9	10	11	12	13	14	15	16	17	18		TOTAL
PAR	POS		4	5	3	4	4	3	5	4	4	4	4	5	3	4	4	3	4	4		TOTAL
Keith Mitchell	T113	Rd 1	4	4	3	4	5	4	6	4	5	4	5	4	3	4	5	3	4	4	75	
USA	**T74**	Rd 2	4	5	3	4	4	3	4	4	4	3	4	5	3	3	4	3	4	5	69	+2 **144**
Takumi Kanaya [a]	T72	Rd 1	4	4	3	5	4	3	5	4	5	4	4	5	3	5	3	3	4	5	73	
Japan	**T74**	Rd 2	4	5	3	4	5	3	4	4	4	3	3	4	3	5	4	4	4	5	71	+2 **144**
Abraham Ancer	T54	Rd 1	5	5	2	4	4	3	5	4	4	4	4	5	3	4	5	3	4	4	72	
Mexico	**T74**	Rd 2	4	5	3	4	4	3	5	4	4	4	5	4	3	4	4	4	4	4	72	+2 **144**
Brandt Snedeker	T94	Rd 1	4	5	3	4	3	3	5	5	5	4	4	5	3	4	4	3	4	6	74	
USA	**T74**	Rd 2	4	7	3	5	4	3	4	4	4	3	4	4	3	4	4	4	3	3	70	+2 **144**
Brian Harman	T54	Rd 1	5	4	3	4	4	3	5	4	4	4	6	5	3	4	4	3	3	4	72	
USA	**T74**	Rd 2	5	4	3	4	4	3	5	4	3	4	5	5	3	4	4	4	4	4	72	+2 **144**
Jason Day	T20	Rd 1	4	5	3	4	3	3	5	4	3	4	4	5	3	4	4	3	4	5	70	
Australia	**T74**	Rd 2	4	4	3	4	4	3	5	4	4	3	4	4	4	6	5	4	5	4	74	+2 **144**
Keegan Bradley	T72	Rd 1	4	4	3	4	5	3	4	4	5	5	4	6	3	4	4	4	3	4	73	
USA	**T74**	Rd 2	5	5	3	3	4	3	5	4	4	4	4	3	4	4	3	4	5	71		+2 **144**
James Sugrue [a]	T42	Rd 1	4	4	3	4	4	2	5	5	4	3	5	4	3	4	4	4	5	4	71	
Republic of Ireland	**T74**	Rd 2	4	5	2	4	4	4	5	3	4	4	5	4	3	7	4	3	4	4	73	+2 **144**

HOLE			1	2	3	4	5	6	7	8	9	10	11	12	13	14	15	16	17	18			
PAR		POS	4	5	3	4	4	3	5	4	4	4	4	5	3	4	4	3	4	4			TOTAL
Alex Levy	T72	Rd 1	4	5	3	4	3	3	5	4	5	4	5	5	2	4	4	4	4	5	73		
France	**T74**	Rd 2	3	6	2	4	3	3	5	4	5	4	5	5	3	5	5	3	3	3	71	+2	**144**
Andrew Johnston	T72	Rd 1	4	3	3	5	4	3	4	4	5	4	4	6	3	5	5	3	4	4	73		
England	**T74**	Rd 2	5	6	3	5	4	2	5	3	3	4	4	5	3	6	4	2	3	4	71	+2	**144**
Connor Syme	T54	Rd 1	3	5	3	4	4	3	5	4	4	4	4	4	3	6	5	3	4	4	72		
Scotland	**T74**	Rd 2	4	5	4	4	3	3	4	4	4	4	5	4	4	4	4	3	4	5	72	+2	**144**
Rory McIlroy	T150	Rd 1	8	5	4	4	4	3	4	4	3	4	4	5	3	4	4	5	4	7	79		
Northern Ireland	**T74**	Rd 2	4	5	2	4	4	3	4	4	4	3	3	4	4	3	4	2	4	4	65	+2	**144**
Nate Lashley	T113	Rd 1	4	5	3	4	3	4	6	4	4	5	5	4	3	4	5	3	5	4	75		
USA	**T74**	Rd 2	4	5	3	4	4	4	6	4	4	3	4	4	2	5	4	2	3	4	69	+2	**144**
Chris Wood	T72	Rd 1	3	5	4	4	4	3	5	5	5	4	5	4	3	4	5	3	4	4	73		
England	**T87**	Rd 2	4	5	3	5	4	3	5	4	4	4	4	4	3	5	3	3	5	4	72	+3	**145**
Kurt Kitayama	T94	Rd 1	4	5	3	5	4	4	5	4	4	4	4	4	3	4	5	4	3	5	74		
USA	**T87**	Rd 2	4	5	2	3	4	3	4	3	4	5	4	4	3	5	4	4	4	6	71	+3	**145**
Dongkyu Jang	T128	Rd 1	5	5	3	4	4	3	5	5	4	4	4	7	3	4	5	3	3	5	76		
Korea	**T87**	Rd 2	4	4	3	4	4	3	5	5	3	4	4	5	3	3	4	3	4	4	69	+3	**145**
Chez Reavie	T72	Rd 1	4	4	4	5	3	3	5	5	4	3	5	5	2	5	4	4	3	5	73		
USA	**T87**	Rd 2	4	5	3	5	5	3	4	5	5	4	4	3	4	4	3	3	3	4	72	+3	**145**
Adrian Otaegui	T72	Rd 1	4	5	4	4	4	3	5	4	4	4	4	5	3	4	4	4	4	4	73		
Spain	**T87**	Rd 2	5	5	3	4	4	3	4	4	4	5	3	5	3	4	4	3	4	4	72	+3	**145**
Darren Clarke	T42	Rd 1	3	5	2	4	3	3	6	4	4	4	5	4	3	5	3	4	5	4	71		
Northern Ireland	**T87**	Rd 2	4	5	2	4	4	3	5	5	5	4	4	3	5	3	3	4	7		74	+3	**145**
Christiaan Bezuidenhout	T94	Rd 1	4	5	3	6	4	3	5	4	3	4	5	3	5	5	2	5	4		74		
South Africa	**T87**	Rd 2	4	4	2	4	4	3	4	4	5	4	6	5	3	4	3	3	5	4	71	+3	**145**
Padraig Harrington	T113	Rd 1	4	5	2	4	3	4	5	5	5	4	5	3	4	6	3	3	5		75		
Republic of Ireland	**T87**	Rd 2	4	4	3	4	4	2	4	5	4	4	4	4	5	3	3	4	4		70	+3	**145**
Gary Woodland	T94	Rd 1	4	5	3	4	3	4	6	4	4	4	4	5	3	4	4	3	5	4	74		
USA	**T87**	Rd 2	4	5	3	4	4	3	5	3	4	4	4	5	2	5	4	3	5	4	71	+3	**145**
Hideki Matsuyama	T42	Rd 1	5	4	3	5	4	4	5	4	4	3	4	5	3	4	4	3	4	3	71		
Japan	**T87**	Rd 2	7	4	3	4	4	3	4	4	4	5	5	5	2	5	4	3	4	4	74	+3	**145**
Si Woo Kim	T20	Rd 1	4	4	3	4	4	3	4	5	4	4	4	4	3	4	4	4	4	4	70		
Korea	**T87**	Rd 2	4	4	4	5	4	3	5	5	4	5	4	5	2	4	4	3	5	5	75	+3	**145**
David Lipsky	T94	Rd 1	5	4	3	4	4	3	5	4	4	4	5	5	3	5	4	3	4	5	74		
USA	**T98**	Rd 2	3	6	3	5	4	3	5	4	4	4	4	6	4	4	3	2	4	4	72	+4	**146**
Patton Kizzire	T72	Rd 1	4	4	3	4	3	4	5	4	4	6	4	3	5	5	3	4	4		73		
USA	**T98**	Rd 2	4	5	2	4	4	3	5	5	4	4	4	4	5	4	4	4	4		73	+4	**146**
Yoshinori Fujimoto	T113	Rd 1	6	5	3	5	4	3	5	4	3	4	4	5	4	4	5	3	4	4	75		
Japan	**T98**	Rd 2	5	6	3	4	3	2	3	5	3	3	5	5	3	5	4	3	4	5	71	+4	**146**
Doyeob Mun	T94	Rd 1	4	4	3	4	3	3	5	4	4	4	5	5	4	4	5	4	4	5	74		
Korea	**T98**	Rd 2	4	5	3	4	3	3	4	5	5	4	4	6	3	4	4	3	4	4	72	+4	**146**
Sung Kang	T94	Rd 1	4	5	4	4	4	3	5	4	4	4	4	4	5	5	3	4	4		74		
Korea	**T98**	Rd 2	4	5	3	5	4	3	4	4	3	4	6	5	4	3	3	4	4		72	+4	**146**
Haotong Li	T94	Rd 1	4	5	2	4	4	4	6	3	5	4	5	3	5	4	4	4	3		74		
China	**T98**	Rd 2	5	5	3	4	4	2	5	4	4	5	6	4	3	4	3	3	4	4	72	+4	**146**
Zach Johnson	T94	Rd 1	5	5	3	3	4	4	5	4	4	4	5	4	4	4	4	4	4	4	74		
USA	**T98**	Rd 2	4	5	2	4	3	2	5	4	5	4	4	5	3	5	3	4	5	5	72	+4	**146**

HOLE			1	2	3	4	5	6	7	8	9	10	11	12	13	14	15	16	17	18		TOTAL
PAR	POS		4	5	3	4	4	3	5	4	4	4	5	3	4	4	3	4	4	4		TOTAL
Matthew Baldwin	T144	Rd 1	7	5	3	3	5	4	5	4	4	4	5	5	3	4	4	3	4	6	78	
England	T98	Rd 2	4	6	4	4	3	2	5	4	4	4	3	4	3	4	3	3	4	4	68	+4 **146**
Jack Senior	T113	Rd 1	4	5	2	4	4	4	5	4	4	3	4	5	4	5	4	4	5	5	75	
England	T98	Rd 2	3	5	4	4	3	3	4	5	4	4	4	4	3	4	6	3	4	4	71	+4 **146**
Joaquin Niemann	T128	Rd 1	4	4	3	4	4	6	5	4	5	4	4	5	3	5	4	3	5	4	76	
Chile	T107	Rd 2	5	5	3	4	4	3	5	4	5	4	4	4	2	5	4	3	3	3	71	+5 **147**
Jake McLeod	T128	Rd 1	4	5	3	5	4	4	5	5	5	4	4	5	3	4	6	2	4	4	76	
Australia	T107	Rd 2	5	5	2	4	3	4	4	4	4	5	5	5	2	3	4	4	4	4	71	+5 **147**
Billy Horschel	T128	Rd 1	4	5	3	5	4	3	6	3	4	5	4	5	3	5	4	4	5	4	76	
USA	T107	Rd 2	4	4	3	5	4	4	3	4	5	4	4	4	3	6	4	3	3	4	71	+5 **147**
Jazz Janewattananond	T94	Rd 1	5	4	3	5	4	3	5	4	5	4	5	6	3	4	4	3	4	3	74	
Thailand	T107	Rd 2	4	4	3	4	4	3	5	4	4	5	4	5	3	4	4	4	3	6	73	+5 **147**
Paul Lawrie	T113	Rd 1	5	4	2	4	4	4	6	4	4	4	4	4	3	5	4	3	5	5	75	
Scotland	T107	Rd 2	3	6	3	4	4	3	6	4	4	4	4	4	3	4	4	4	4	4	72	+5 **147**
Brandon Stone	T54	Rd 1	4	5	3	4	4	3	5	3	4	4	4	3	5	4	3	4	5	5	72	
South Africa	T107	Rd 2	4	4	3	6	4	3	4	4	4	4	5	5	3	4	5	3	4	6	75	+5 **147**
Robert Rock	T128	Rd 1	5	5	4	4	4	3	5	4	4	4	4	5	3	4	4	4	4	6	76	
England	T107	Rd 2	4	5	3	4	3	2	4	5	5	4	3	6	3	5	4	3	4	4	71	+5 **147**
Isidro Benitez	T113	Rd 1	3	4	4	5	4	3	6	4	4	3	4	5	3	4	5	4	4	6	75	
Mexico	T107	Rd 2	3	4	3	6	4	3	5	4	4	5	4	5	3	5	4	4	3	3	72	+5 **147**
Matthias Schmid [a]	T128	Rd 1	5	4	3	4	5	3	4	4	4	5	6	5	3	4	5	3	3	6	76	
Germany	T107	Rd 2	4	4	3	4	4	2	4	4	4	4	7	5	3	5	3	3	4	4	71	+5 **147**
Bryson DeChambeau	T94	Rd 1	4	5	3	4	4	3	6	4	4	3	5	5	3	4	5	4	4	4	74	
USA	T107	Rd 2	4	5	3	4	4	3	6	4	4	4	4	4	3	4	4	5	4	4	73	+5 **147**
Alexander Björk	T140	Rd 1	5	4	3	4	4	3	6	4	4	5	5	6	3	3	4	4	5	5	77	
Sweden	T107	Rd 2	4	5	2	5	4	3	4	4	4	3	4	6	2	4	5	4	3	4	70	+5 **147**
Mikumu Horikawa	T42	Rd 1	5	5	3	4	4	3	5	4	4	4	4	4	2	4	4	4	4	4	71	
Japan	T107	Rd 2	5	5	4	5	4	3	6	5	4	4	3	5	5	4	2	4	4	4	76	+5 **147**
Joel Dahmen	T128	Rd 1	4	4	3	4	4	4	6	4	4	4	4	6	4	4	5	3	4	5	76	
USA	T119	Rd 2	4	4	3	5	5	3	4	4	4	4	3	5	3	5	3	3	5	5	72	+6 **148**
Tiger Woods	T144	Rd 1	4	5	3	4	5	5	6	4	5	5	4	5	3	5	3	3	4	5	78	
USA	T119	Rd 2	3	5	3	4	4	2	6	4	4	3	3	5	3	4	4	3	5	5	70	+6 **148**
Gunn Charoenkul	T54	Rd 1	4	5	2	4	4	3	5	4	5	4	5	5	3	4	4	3	4	4	72	
Thailand	T119	Rd 2	5	5	5	4	4	3	4	4	5	4	5	4	3	5	5	3	4	4	76	+6 **148**
Zander Lombard	T42	Rd 1	4	4	3	4	5	3	5	4	4	5	3	4	3	5	3	3	4	5	71	
South Africa	T119	Rd 2	6	4	2	5	6	3	5	5	5	4	4	5	3	4	4	3	5	4	77	+6 **148**
Rafa Cabrera Bello	T72	Rd 1	5	5	4	4	5	2	5	5	5	3	3	7	3	3	5	3	3	3	73	
Spain	T119	Rd 2	5	5	4	3	3	3	4	4	4	5	6	5	3	7	4	3	3	4	75	+6 **148**
Oliver Wilson	T72	Rd 1	4	4	3	4	4	3	6	4	4	4	4	6	3	4	4	4	4	4	73	
England	T119	Rd 2	4	5	3	4	4	3	7	4	4	5	4	5	3	4	5	3	4	4	75	+6 **148**
Corey Conners	T54	Rd 1	4	4	3	3	4	3	6	4	4	4	4	5	3	4	4	4	4	5	72	
Canada	T119	Rd 2	5	5	2	4	5	3	5	5	4	6	4	5	3	4	4	4	4	4	76	+6 **148**
Jimmy Walker	T94	Rd 1	5	5	3	4	4	2	6	4	5	3	5	5	3	4	4	4	4	4	74	
USA	T119	Rd 2	4	4	3	4	5	3	5	6	5	3	4	5	2	4	4	5	4	4	74	+6 **148**
Jorge Campillo	T128	Rd 1	4	6	3	4	4	4	6	4	5	4	3	5	3	4	4	3	5	5	76	
Spain	T127	Rd 2	4	4	3	4	4	3	4	3	4	4	4	5	4	3	8	5	4	4	3	73	+7 **149**

HOLE			1	2	3	4	5	6	7	8	9	10	11	12	13	14	15	16	17	18		
PAR	POS		4	5	3	4	4	3	5	4	4	4	4	5	3	4	4	3	4	4		TOTAL
Shaun Norris	T72	Rd 1	4	5	3	6	3	3	4	4	4	3	4	5	3	5	4	4	5	4	73	
South Africa	T127	Rd 2	4	5	3	5	4	3	6	3	4	4	5	5	3	7	4	3	3	5	76	+7 **149**
Chan Kim	T113	Rd 1	6	5	3	6	3	3	4	4	4	3	5	4	4	5	4	3	4	5	75	
USA	T127	Rd 2	5	5	3	4	4	3	4	4	4	5	4	3	3	5	5	3	5	5	74	+7 **149**
Brandon Wu (a)	T72	Rd 1	4	5	4	4	4	2	4	4	3	5	4	5	3	5	5	3	4	5	73	
USA	T127	Rd 2	3	7	3	4	4	3	5	5	3	4	7	4	3	5	5	3	4	4	76	+7 **149**
Ryan Palmer	T94	Rd 1	6	6	2	4	2	3	4	4	4	4	5	6	4	3	4	3	5	5	74	
USA	T127	Rd 2	6	5	3	4	4	3	5	4	4	4	6	5	3	5	4	3	4	3	75	+7 **149**
Andrea Pavan	T72	Rd 1	5	5	3	4	4	4	4	3	4	4	4	4	3	4	4	4	6	4	73	
Italy	T127	Rd 2	4	4	4	5	4	2	7	4	4	4	4	6	3	5	3	3	4	6	76	+7 **149**
Ian Poulter	T113	Rd 1	4	4	3	4	4	3	6	4	4	6	5	4	3	4	5	3	5	4	75	
England	T127	Rd 2	4	4	3	4	4	3	4	4	6	4	5	5	3	6	5	2	4	4	74	+7 **149**
Luke List	T72	Rd 1	4	3	3	4	5	3	5	4	4	5	5	5	3	4	4	3	4	5	73	
USA	T127	Rd 2	4	6	3	5	4	3	5	4	4	4	5	4	3	5	4	5	4	4	76	+7 **149**
Adri Arnaus	T113	Rd 1	5	5	3	4	5	3	6	4	4	4	5	4	3	4	5	3	4	4	75	
Spain	T135	Rd 2	6	5	3	4	4	3	4	4	5	4	4	5	3	5	5	3	4	4	75	+8 **150**
Marc Leishman	T144	Rd 1	4	5	3	5	5	3	5	3	5	4	6	7	2	4	4	3	6	4	78	
Australia	T135	Rd 2	4	5	3	4	4	3	4	4	4	5	4	5	3	5	4	3	4	4	72	+8 **150**
Phil Mickelson	T128	Rd 1	4	5	3	5	4	4	4	4	5	4	5	6	3	3	4	4	5	4	76	
USA	T135	Rd 2	4	7	3	3	3	4	5	5	5	4	4	5	3	5	4	3	4	3	74	+8 **150**
Mike Lorenzo-Vera	T140	Rd 1	4	5	3	6	4	3	5	5	4	5	5	5	3	4	5	3	4	4	77	
France	T135	Rd 2	4	5	3	4	4	3	6	6	4	4	3	4	4	4	4	3	4	4	73	+8 **150**
Yuta Ikeda	T128	Rd 1	5	4	3	4	4	4	5	5	4	4	5	5	3	5	4	3	5	4	76	
Japan	T139	Rd 2	4	4	3	4	4	2	6	5	4	4	5	5	3	5	4	4	4	5	75	+9 **151**
Andy Sullivan	T128	Rd 1	6	6	2	4	4	3	5	4	4	4	6	5	2	5	4	3	4	5	76	
England	T139	Rd 2	3	5	4	5	4	4	5	5	4	3	5	5	3	4	4	3	4	5	75	+9 **151**
Richard Sterne	T144	Rd 1	4	5	3	5	4	4	5	4	4	5	4	5	3	4	6	4	4	5	78	
South Africa	T139	Rd 2	4	5	3	5	4	3	3	6	4	4	4	5	3	4	4	4	3	5	73	+9 **151**
CT Pan	T140	Rd 1	6	5	3	4	4	3	5	4	5	4	6	5	3	4	3	4	4	5	77	
Chinese Taipei	T139	Rd 2	4	5	3	4	4	3	7	4	4	4	3	5	3	4	5	4	4	4	74	+9 **151**
Curtis Knipes (a)	T54	Rd 1	4	5	2	5	3	4	5	3	4	4	5	4	4	4	4	4	4	4	72	
England	T139	Rd 2	7	6	3	4	4	3	5	4	4	5	6	5	3	4	5	3	4	4	79	+9 **151**
Sungjae Im	T42	Rd 1	3	4	3	4	4	4	5	5	4	4	4	5	3	4	4	3	4	4	71	
Korea	T139	Rd 2	4	5	3	4	6	3	4	4	5	4	4	5	3	5	5	3	8	5	80	+9 **151**
Adam Scott	T144	Rd 1	4	7	2	4	4	3	6	4	5	4	4	5	4	4	5	3	6	4	78	
Australia	T139	Rd 2	5	4	2	4	4	3	5	5	5	4	4	5	3	4	3	3	4	6	73	+9 **151**
Emiliano Grillo	T72	Rd 1	4	4	3	4	7	4	4	3	5	4	4	5	1	5	5	3	4	4	73	
Argentina	T146	Rd 2	5	5	3	4	4	3	5	5	4	4	5	5	4	5	4	6	4	4	79	+10 **152**
Sam Locke	T113	Rd 1	5	4	4	5	4	3	5	3	6	4	5	6	3	4	4	3	4	3	75	
Scotland	T146	Rd 2	5	5	3	4	4	4	5	4	5	4	4	6	3	4	6	3	4	4	77	+10 **152**
Shugo Imahira	T153	Rd 1	4	6	4	8	3	4	6	5	5	4	4	5	3	4	5	3	5	5	83	
Japan	T146	Rd 2	4	5	3	4	5	2	4	4	5	4	4	4	3	4	3	3	4	4	69	+10 **152**
Garrick Porteous	T150	Rd 1	4	5	3	4	4	4	4	5	4	4	8	4	4	6	3	4	5	4	79	
England	T146	Rd 2	4	4	3	4	5	2	6	5	4	5	4	4	3	6	3	3	4	4	73	+10 **152**
Tom Lehman	T144	Rd 1	5	5	3	4	3	4	5	5	4	3	5	5	4	4	5	3	6	5	78	
USA	T150	Rd 2	5	5	4	5	4	5	5	4	4	3	4	5	3	4	4	4	4	4	76	+12 **154**

HOLE			1	2	3	4	5	6	7	8	9	10	11	12	13	14	15	16	17	18	
PAR	POS		4	5	3	4	4	3	5	4	4	4	5	3	4	4	3	4	4		TOTAL
Austin Connelly	T113	Rd 1	4	5	3	4	4	3	6	4	7	4	5	4	2	5	4	3	4	4	75
Canada	**T150**	Rd 2	5	6	2	6	4	3	5	5	4	5	4	5	5	5	4	3	4	4	79 +12 **154**
Prom Meesawat	T72	Rd 1	4	4	4	5	4	3	5	4	3	4	4	6	3	4	4	3	4	5	73
Thailand	**T150**	Rd 2	5	5	3	5	4	3	6	4	5	5	4	5	4	5	5	3	6	4	81 +12 **154**
Miguel Ángel Jiménez	152	Rd 1	4	5	4	5	4	3	5	5	6	5	4	5	5	4	5	4	4	5	82
Spain	**T153**	Rd 2	4	5	3	5	4	3	4	4	4	5	4	5	3	4	4	3	4	5	73 +13 **155**
Dimitrios Papadatos	T153	Rd 1	4	6	3	5	5	3	6	4	6	4	5	5	5	5	5	3	6	3	83
Australia	**T153**	Rd 2	4	5	3	4	5	4	5	3	5	4	4	5	3	5	3	3	3	4	72 +13 **155**
Thomas Thurloway[a]	T153	Rd 1	4	5	3	5	7	4	6	5	4	4	4	5	3	5	4	3	6	6	83
England	**155**	Rd 2	4	4	4	5	5	2	5	3	4	4	5	5	3	4	4	3	4	5	73 +14 **156**
David Duval	156	Rd 1	3	4	3	4	8	4	14	4	5	5	5	5	3	4	5	4	7	4	91
USA	**156**	Rd 2	5	8	3	5	5	3	5	6	4	3	4	5	3	5	4	3	3	4	78 +27 **169**

THE TOP TENS

Driving Distance

1 **Ryan Fox**.................. 315.8
2 Dustin Johnson 308.6
3 Callum Shinkwin 308.0
4 Tyrrell Hatton 306.3
5 JB Holmes 305.0
6 Bubba Watson........... 304.5
7 Lucas Bjerregaard 304.0
8 Byeong Hun An......... 303.5
9 Romain Langasque 301.9
10 Tony Finau 301.4
12 *Shane Lowry 301.1*

Fairways Hit
Maximum of 56

1 **Paul Waring** 44
2 Adam Hadwin 42
3 Lucas Glover 41
4 Lee Westwood............... 40
4 Henrik Stenson............... 40
4 Kevin Streelman 40
4 Yosuke Asaji 40
8 Tyrrell Hatton.................39
8 Mikko Korhonen.............39
8 JB Holmes 39
22 *Shane Lowry.....................35*

Greens in Regulation
Maximum of 72

1 *Shane Lowry*....................57
2 Francesco Molinari......... 56
3 Tony Finau 54
3 Lee Westwood............... 54
5 Tyrrell Hatton.................53
5 Rickie Fowler..................53
5 Rory Sabbatini................53
5 Louis Oosthuizen 53
9 Tom Lewis 52
9 Xander Schauffele 52

Putts

1 Sang Hyun Park............ 112
1 Bernd Wiesberger........ 112
1 Kyle Stanley 112
1 Justin Harding 112
5 Danny Willett.................113
5 Henrik Stenson...............113
5 Ernie Els.........................113
8 Robert MacIntyre.......... 114
8 Justin Thomas............... 114
8 Justin Rose.................... 114
8 Kiradech Aphibarnrat ... 114
22 *Shane Lowry...................117*

Statistical Rankings

	Driving Distance	Rank	Fairways Hit	Rank	Greens In Regulation	Rank	Putts	Rank
Byeong Hun An	303.5	8	27	66	48	25	118	28
Kiradech Aphibarnrat	293.8	30	29	61	44	58	114	8
Yosuke Asaji	276.3	68	40	4	46	40	119	39
Nino Bertasio	280.3	65	30	55	42	68	119	39
Lucas Bjerregaard	304.0	7	30	55	46	40	116	16
Patrick Cantlay	297.9	21	26	68	51	11	128	72
Paul Casey	289.1	48	31	46	50	13	127	71
Stewart Cink	289.9	45	33	35	47	34	116	16
Ernie Els	285.8	54	34	30	41	72	113	5
Tony Finau	301.4	10	30	55	54	3	120	46
Matthew Fitzpatrick	299.4	13	33	35	47	34	117	22
Tommy Fleetwood	289.1	48	36	16	50	13	115	12
Rickie Fowler	283.9	57	37	12	53	5	116	16
Ryan Fox	315.8	1	35	22	50	13	117	22
Dylan Frittelli	293.8	30	37	12	44	58	118	28
Jim Furyk	269.1	72	36	16	45	51	118	28
Sergio Garcia	298.0	20	31	46	44	58	121	52
Lucas Glover	296.6	23	41	3	46	40	118	28
Branden Grace	284.6	56	32	42	46	40	122	56
Adam Hadwin	291.0	37	42	2	48	25	122	56
Justin Harding	290.8	38	31	46	42	68	112	1
Tyrrell Hatton	306.3	4	39	8	53	5	119	39
Benjamin Hebert	286.0	53	36	16	46	40	119	39
Charley Hoffman	299.0	16	34	29	46	39	119	39
JB Holmes	305.0	5	39	8	46	40	119	39
Innchoon Hwang	283.5	60	33	35	51	11	123	61
Yuki Inamori	279.4	66	36	16	50	13	128	72
Dustin Johnson	308.6	2	30	55	46	40	123	61
Kevin Kisner	275.8	69	34	30	50	13	122	56
Russell Knox	291.8	35	38	11	44	58	118	28
Brooks Koepka	299.3	14	36	16	47	34	116	16
Jason Kokrak	298.6	18	29	61	48	25	125	69
Mikko Korhonen	292.0	34	39	8	46	40	122	56
Matt Kuchar	278.9	67	33	35	50	13	122	56
Romain Langasque	301.9	9	26	68	44	58	118	28
Tom Lewis	294.1	29	37	12	52	9	123	61
Shane Lowry	301.1	12	35	22	57	1	117	22
Joost Luiten	295.9	25	37	12	48	25	120	46
Robert MacIntyre	299.1	15	26	68	49	22	114	8
Graeme McDowell	274.9	70	24	71	50	13	121	52
Francesco Molinari	283.3	61	28	64	56	2	124	67
Alex Noren	295.0	26	35	22	48	25	118	28
Thorbjørn Olesen	291.3	36	31	46	45	51	121	52
Louis Oosthuizen	296.6	23	31	46	53	5	126	70
Sang Hyun Park	290.1	42	35	22	43	65	112	1
Eddie Pepperell	290.0	44	32	42	39	73	115	12
Thomas Pieters	297.9	21	28	64	47	34	120	46
Andrew Putnam	288.5	50	35	22	45	51	118	28
Jon Rahm	301.3	11	31	46	50	13	117	22
Doc Redman	290.6	39	31	46	45	51	115	12
Patrick Reed	283.6	59	31	46	47	34	115	12
Justin Rose	298.4	19	33	35	43	65	114	8
Rory Sabbatini	290.3	41	35	22	53	5	123	61
Xander Schauffele	294.9	27	31	46	52	9	123	61
Shubhankar Sharma	289.3	47	35	22	48	25	120	46
Callum Shinkwin	308.0	3	30	55	49	22	119	39
Webb Simpson	283.3	61	34	30	46	40	117	22
Cameron Smith	293.6	32	34	30	49	22	120	46
Jordan Spieth	294.9	27	22	73	46	40	116	16
Kyle Stanley	285.5	55	36	16	42	68	112	1
Henrik Stenson	263.5	73	40	4	44	58	113	5
Kevin Streelman	289.4	46	40	4	45	51	117	22
Justin Thomas	288.4	51	23	72	48	25	114	8
Ashton Turner	272.9	71	30	55	48	25	124	67
Erik van Rooyen	293.5	33	33	35	45	51	118	28
Matthew Wallace	282.5	63	34	30	46	40	121	52
Paul Waring	283.8	58	44	1	43	65	118	28
Bubba Watson	304.5	6	32	42	48	25	123	61
Lee Westwood	298.8	17	40	4	54	3	120	46
Bernd Wiesberger	281.3	64	32	42	42	68	112	1
Danny Willett	290.1	42	29	61	50	13	113	5
Andrew Wilson	290.4	40	27	66	44	58	116	16
Aaron Wise	286.6	52	33	35	45	51	118	28

Name	Driving Distance	Rank	Fairways Hit	Rank	Greens In Regulation	Rank	Putts	Rank
Abraham Ancer	287.3	110	19	30	24	60	62	101
Adri Arnaus	304.0	19	17	63	22	94	64	128
Matthew Baldwin	269.0	150	13	130	24	60	59	51
Isidro Benitez	288.8	100	19	30	24	60	61	81
C Bezuidenhout	288.0	103	14	118	23	74	59	51
Alexander Björk	280.3	129	16	77	17	147	56	12
Keegan Bradley	300.5	34	15	96	25	40	65	141
Rafa Cabrera Bello	286.3	114	15	96	20	124	58	32
Jorge Campillo	269.3	149	17	63	23	74	65	141
Gunn Charoenkul	295.3	65	15	96	23	74	62	101
Darren Clarke	297.8	52	20	18	21	110	54	5
Austin Connelly	266.5	152	14	118	24	60	69	154
Corey Conners	284.3	123	21	10	23	74	64	128
Joel Dahmen	296.5	61	16	77	21	112	62	101
Jason Day	271.8	144	13	129	20	123	55	8
Bryson DeChambeau	292.3	74	20	19	22	94	61	81
David Duval	264.3	153	9	156	16	151	62	101
Yoshinori Fujimoto	287.8	104	13	130	20	124	58	32
Emiliano Grillo	294.5	68	16	77	18	142	59	51
Brian Harman	289.8	91	23	2	27	14	65	141
Padraig Harrington	311.0	6	16	77	24	60	64	128
Mikumu Horikawa	271.8	144	18	44	23	74	63	119
Billy Horschel	290.8	83	19	30	26	24	65	141
Yuta Ikeda	287.5	107	11	149	21	112	62	101
Sungjae Im	299.3	38	16	77	17	147	60	64
Shugo Imahira	281.3	126	20	19	22	94	63	119
J Janewattananond	290.8	83	20	19	26	24	68	151
Dongkyu Jang	284.8	120	16	77	23	74	62	101
Miguel Ángel Jiménez	271.5	147	11	149	18	142	61	81
Zach Johnson	273.3	142	15	96	15	153	52	1
Andrew Johnston	297.0	56	18	44	23	74	61	81
Takumi Kanaya [a]	299.0	40	23	2	21	112	60	64
Sung Kang	313.5	4	14	118	23	74	61	81
Chan Kim	309.5	7	13	130	19	132	61	81
Si Woo Kim	287.5	107	20	19	19	132	56	12
Kurt Kitayama	317.0	2	16	77	27	14	69	154
Patton Kizzire	290.8	83	16	77	19	132	62	101
Curtis Knipes [a]	253.3	156	13	130	14	155	56	12
Nate Lashley	289.0	97	14	118	17	147	55	8
Paul Lawrie	268.3	151	14	118	20	124	63	119
Tom Lehman	275.0	139	15	96	16	151	60	64
Marc Leishman	298.5	47	17	63	25	40	68	151
Alex Levy	303.0	23	14	118	23	74	63	119
Haotong Li	278.8	131	15	96	17	147	54	5
David Lipsky	303.5	20	14	118	23	74	62	101
Luke List	316.0	3	17	63	21	112	64	128
Sam Locke	302.0	27	12	147	19	132	64	128
Zander Lombard	308.8	8	13	130	19	132	62	101
Mike Lorenzo-Vera	275.8	138	13	130	20	124	62	101
Hideki Matsuyama	297.5	53	15	96	26	24	63	119
Rory McIlroy	290.0	87	18	44	25	40	59	51
Jake McLeod	289.8	91	14	118	25	40	66	147
Prom Meesawat	271.5	147	15	96	19	132	67	149
Phil Mickelson	302.0	27	15	96	18	142	61	81
Keith Mitchell	303.3	21	19	30	26	24	62	101
Doyeob Mun	298.8	42	15	96	19	132	57	24
Joaquin Niemann	300.0	37	18	44	21	112	60	64
Shaun Norris	307.0	12	13	130	21	112	59	51
Adrian Otaegui	295.0	66	20	19	25	40	64	128
Ryan Palmer	301.8	29	16	77	19	132	57	24
CT Pan	274.0	141	16	77	19	132	61	81
Dimitrios Papadatos	297.5	53	14	118	22	94	66	147
Andrea Pavan	295.5	64	13	130	22	94	62	101
Garrick Porteous	286.0	116	18	44	23	74	64	128
Ian Poulter	298.8	42	16	77	22	94	64	128
Chez Reavie	293.0	73	16	77	22	94	61	81
Robert Rock	290.0	87	17	63	24	60	62	101
Matthias Schmid [a]	323.8	1	13	130	22	94	60	64
Adam Scott	290.3	86	13	130	22	94	65	141
Jack Senior	304.8	16	15	96	15	153	52	1
Brandt Snedeker	296.0	62	20	19	23	74	59	51
Richard Sterne	301.0	32	20	19	26	24	69	154
Brandon Stone	291.3	80	16	77	28	4	68	151
James Sugrue [a]	298.5	47	18	44	19	132	57	24
Andy Sullivan	291.8	76	15	96	21	112	63	119
Connor Syme	284.5	121	14	118	21	112	58	32
Thomas Thurloway [a]	298.0	51	11	149	13	156	59	51
Jimmy Walker	287.5	107	16	77	21	112	61	81
Oliver Wilson	289.5	95	15	96	18	142	58	32
Chris Wood	262.3	155	12	147	18	142	54	5
Gary Woodland	299.3	38	18	44	20	124	59	51
Tiger Woods	280.8	128	17	63	24	60	64	128
Brandon Wu [a]	304.5	18	13	130	22	94	62	101

Roll of Honour

Year	Champion	Score	Margin	Runners-up	Venue
1860	Willie Park Sr	174	2	Tom Morris Sr	Prestwick
1861	Tom Morris Sr	163	4	Willie Park Sr	Prestwick
1862	Tom Morris Sr	163	13	Willie Park Sr	Prestwick
1863	Willie Park Sr	168	2	Tom Morris Sr	Prestwick
1864	Tom Morris Sr	167	2	Andrew Strath	Prestwick
1865	Andrew Strath	162	2	Willie Park Sr	Prestwick
1866	Willie Park Sr	169	2	David Park	Prestwick
1867	Tom Morris Sr	170	2	Willie Park Sr	Prestwick
1868	Tommy Morris Jr	154	3	Tom Morris Sr	Prestwick
1869	Tommy Morris Jr	157	11	Bob Kirk	Prestwick
1870	Tommy Morris Jr	149	12	Bob Kirk, Davie Strath	Prestwick
1871	*No Championship*				
1872	Tommy Morris Jr	166	3	Davie Strath	Prestwick
1873	Tom Kidd	179	1	Jamie Anderson	St Andrews
1874	Mungo Park	159	2	Tommy Morris Jr	Musselburgh
1875	Willie Park Sr	166	2	Bob Martin	Prestwick
1876	Bob Martin	176	—	Davie Strath	St Andrews
	(Martin was awarded the title when Strath refused to play-off)				
1877	Jamie Anderson	160	2	Bob Pringle	Musselburgh
1878	Jamie Anderson	157	2	Bob Kirk	Prestwick
1879	Jamie Anderson	169	3	Jamie Allan, Andrew Kirkaldy	St Andrews
1880	Bob Ferguson	162	5	Peter Paxton	Musselburgh
1881	Bob Ferguson	170	3	Jamie Anderson	Prestwick
1882	Bob Ferguson	171	3	Willie Fernie	St Andrews
1883	Willie Fernie	158	Play-off	Bob Ferguson	Musselburgh
1884	Jack Simpson	160	4	Douglas Rolland, Willie Fernie	Prestwick
1885	Bob Martin	171	1	Archie Simpson	St Andrews
1886	David Brown	157	2	Willie Campbell	Musselburgh
1887	Willie Park Jr	161	1	Bob Martin	Prestwick
1888	Jack Burns	171	1	David Anderson Jr, Ben Sayers	St Andrews
1889	Willie Park Jr	155	Play-off	Andrew Kirkaldy	Musselburgh
1890	John Ball Jr[a]	164	3	Willie Fernie, Archie Simpson	Prestwick
1891	Hugh Kirkaldy	166	2	Willie Fernie, Andrew Kirkaldy	St Andrews
	(From 1892 the Championship was extended to 72 holes)				
1892	Harold Hilton[a]	305	3	John Ball Jr[a], Hugh Kirkaldy, Sandy Herd	Muirfield
1893	Willie Auchterlonie	322	2	John Laidlay[a]	Prestwick

Fred Daly (1947)

Max Faulkner (1951)

Padraig Harrington (2007, 2008)

Year	Champion	Score	Margin	Runners-up	Venue
1894	JH Taylor	326	5	Douglas Rolland	St George's
1895	JH Taylor	322	4	Sandy Herd	St Andrews
1896	Harry Vardon	316	Play-off	JH Taylor	Muirfield
1897	Harold Hilton[a]	314	1	James Braid	Royal Liverpool
1898	Harry Vardon	307	1	Willie Park Jr	Prestwick
1899	Harry Vardon	310	5	Jack White	St George's
1900	JH Taylor	309	8	Harry Vardon	St Andrews
1901	James Braid	309	3	Harry Vardon	Muirfield
1902	Sandy Herd	307	1	Harry Vardon, James Braid	Royal Liverpool
1903	Harry Vardon	300	6	Tom Vardon	Prestwick
1904	Jack White	296	1	James Braid, JH Taylor	Royal St George's
1905	James Braid	318	5	JH Taylor, Rowland Jones	St Andrews
1906	James Braid	300	4	JH Taylor	Muirfield
1907	Arnaud Massy	312	2	JH Taylor	Royal Liverpool
1908	James Braid	291	8	Tom Ball	Prestwick
1909	JH Taylor	295	6	James Braid, Tom Ball	Cinque Ports
1910	James Braid	299	4	Sandy Herd	St Andrews
1911	Harry Vardon	303	Play-off	Arnaud Massy	Royal St George's
1912	Ted Ray	295	4	Harry Vardon	Muirfield
1913	JH Taylor	304	8	Ted Ray	Royal Liverpool
1914	Harry Vardon	306	3	JH Taylor	Prestwick
1915-1919 No Championship					
1920	George Duncan	303	2	Sandy Herd	Royal Cinque Ports
1921	Jock Hutchison	296	Play-off	Roger Wethered[a]	St Andrews
1922	Walter Hagen	300	1	George Duncan, Jim Barnes	Royal St George's
1923	Arthur Havers	295	1	Walter Hagen	Troon
1924	Walter Hagen	301	1	Ernest Whitcombe	Royal Liverpool
1925	Jim Barnes	300	1	Archie Compston, Ted Ray	Prestwick
1926	Bobby Jones[a]	291	2	Al Watrous	Royal Lytham
1927	Bobby Jones[a]	285	6	Aubrey Boomer, Fred Robson	St Andrews
1928	Walter Hagen	292	2	Gene Sarazen	Royal St George's
1929	Walter Hagen	292	6	Johnny Farrell	Muirfield
1930	Bobby Jones[a]	291	2	Leo Diegel, Macdonald Smith	Royal Liverpool
1931	Tommy Armour	296	1	Jose Jurado	Carnoustie

Year	Champion	Score	Margin	Runners-up	Venue
1932	Gene Sarazen	283	5	Macdonald Smith	Prince's
1933	Denny Shute	292	Play-off	Craig Wood	St Andrews
1934	Henry Cotton	283	5	Sid Brews	Royal St George's
1935	Alf Perry	283	4	Alf Padgham	Muirfield
1936	Alf Padgham	287	1	Jimmy Adams	Royal Liverpool
1937	Henry Cotton	290	2	Reg Whitcombe	Carnoustie
1938	Reg Whitcombe	295	2	Jimmy Adams	Royal St George's
1939	Dick Burton	290	2	Johnny Bulla	St Andrews
1940-1945 No Championship					
1946	Sam Snead	290	4	Bobby Locke, Johnny Bulla	St Andrews
1947	Fred Daly	293	1	Reg Horne, Frank Stranahan[a]	Royal Liverpool
1948	Henry Cotton	284	5	Fred Daly	Muirfield
1949	Bobby Locke	283	Play-off	Harry Bradshaw	Royal St George's
1950	Bobby Locke	279	2	Roberto de Vicenzo	Troon
1951	Max Faulkner	285	2	Antonio Cerda	Royal Portrush
1952	Bobby Locke	287	1	Peter Thomson	Royal Lytham
1953	Ben Hogan	282	4	Frank Stranahan[a], Dai Rees, Peter Thomson, Antonio Cerda	Carnoustie
1954	Peter Thomson	283	1	Syd Scott, Dai Rees, Bobby Locke	Royal Birkdale
1955	Peter Thomson	281	2	John Fallon	St Andrews
1956	Peter Thomson	286	3	Flory Van Donck	Royal Liverpool
1957	Bobby Locke	279	3	Peter Thomson	St Andrews
1958	Peter Thomson	278	Play-off	Dave Thomas	Royal Lytham
1959	Gary Player	284	2	Flory Van Donck, Fred Bullock	Muirfield
1960	Kel Nagle	278	1	Arnold Palmer	St Andrews
1961	Arnold Palmer	284	1	Dai Rees	Royal Birkdale
1962	Arnold Palmer	276	6	Kel Nagle	Troon

(Prior to 1963, scores assessed against "level 4s". From 1963, pars were introduced and holes were played in 3, 4 or 5 shots.)

Year	Champion	To Par	Score	Margin	Runners-up	Venue
1963	Bob Charles	-3	277	Play-off	Phil Rodgers	Royal Lytham
1964	Tony Lema	-9	279	5	Jack Nicklaus	St Andrews
1965	Peter Thomson	-7	285	2	Christy O'Connor Sr, Brian Huggett	Royal Birkdale
1966	Jack Nicklaus	-2	282	1	Dave Thomas, Doug Sanders	Muirfield
1967	Roberto de Vicenzo	-10	278	2	Jack Nicklaus	Royal Liverpool
1968	Gary Player	+1	289	2	Jack Nicklaus, Bob Charles	Carnoustie
1969	Tony Jacklin	-4	280	2	Bob Charles	Royal Lytham
1970	Jack Nicklaus	-5	283	Play-off	Doug Sanders	St Andrews
1971	Lee Trevino	-14	278	1	Liang Huan Lu	Royal Birkdale
1972	Lee Trevino	-6	278	1	Jack Nicklaus	Muirfield
1973	Tom Weiskopf	-12	276	3	Neil Coles, Johnny Miller	Troon
1974	Gary Player	-2	282	4	Peter Oosterhuis	Royal Lytham
1975	Tom Watson	-9	279	Play-off	Jack Newton	Carnoustie
1976	Johnny Miller	-9	279	6	Jack Nicklaus, Seve Ballesteros	Royal Birkdale
1977	Tom Watson	-12	268	1	Jack Nicklaus	Turnberry
1978	Jack Nicklaus	-7	281	2	Simon Owen, Ben Crenshaw, Ray Floyd, Tom Kite	St Andrews
1979	Seve Ballesteros	-1	283	3	Jack Nicklaus, Ben Crenshaw	Royal Lytham
1980	Tom Watson	-13	271	4	Lee Trevino	Muirfield
1981	Bill Rogers	-4	276	4	Bernhard Langer	Royal St George's
1982	Tom Watson	-4	284	1	Peter Oosterhuis, Nick Price	Royal Troon
1983	Tom Watson	-9	275	1	Hale Irwin, Andy Bean	Royal Birkdale
1984	Seve Ballesteros	-12	276	2	Bernhard Langer, Tom Watson	St Andrews

Darren Clarke (2011)   *Rory McIlroy (2014)*   *Shane Lowry (2019)*

Year	Champion	To Par	Score	Margin	Runners-up	Venue
1985	Sandy Lyle	+2	282	1	Payne Stewart	Royal St George's
1986	Greg Norman	E	280	5	Gordon J Brand	Turnberry
1987	Nick Faldo	-5	279	1	Rodger Davis, Paul Azinger	Muirfield
1988	Seve Ballesteros	-11	273	2	Nick Price	Royal Lytham
1989	Mark Calcavecchia	-13	275	Play-off	Greg Norman, Wayne Grady	Royal Troon
1990	Nick Faldo	-18	270	5	Mark McNulty, Payne Stewart	St Andrews
1991	Ian Baker-Finch	-8	272	2	Mike Harwood	Royal Birkdale
1992	Nick Faldo	-12	272	1	John Cook	Muirfield
1993	Greg Norman	-13	267	2	Nick Faldo	Royal St George's
1994	Nick Price	-12	268	1	Jesper Parnevik	Turnberry
1995	John Daly	-6	282	Play-off	Costantino Rocca	St Andrews
1996	Tom Lehman	-13	271	2	Mark McCumber, Ernie Els	Royal Lytham
1997	Justin Leonard	-12	272	3	Jesper Parnevik, Darren Clarke	Royal Troon
1998	Mark O'Meara	E	280	Play-off	Brian Watts	Royal Birkdale
1999	Paul Lawrie	+6	290	Play-off	Justin Leonard, Jean van de Velde	Carnoustie
2000	Tiger Woods	-19	269	8	Ernie Els, Thomas Bjørn	St Andrews
2001	David Duval	-10	274	3	Niclas Fasth	Royal Lytham
2002	Ernie Els	-6	278	Play-off	Thomas Levet, Stuart Appleby, Steve Elkington	Muirfield
2003	Ben Curtis	-1	283	1	Thomas Bjørn, Vijay Singh	Royal St George's
2004	Todd Hamilton	-10	274	Play-off	Ernie Els	Royal Troon
2005	Tiger Woods	-14	274	5	Colin Montgomerie	St Andrews
2006	Tiger Woods	-18	270	2	Chris DiMarco	Royal Liverpool
2007	Padraig Harrington	-7	277	Play-off	Sergio Garcia	Carnoustie
2008	Padraig Harrington	+3	283	4	Ian Poulter	Royal Birkdale
2009	Stewart Cink	-2	278	Play-off	Tom Watson	Turnberry
2010	Louis Oosthuizen	-16	272	7	Lee Westwood	St Andrews
2011	Darren Clarke	-5	275	3	Phil Mickelson, Dustin Johnson	Royal St George's
2012	Ernie Els	-7	273	1	Adam Scott	Royal Lytham
2013	Phil Mickelson	-3	281	3	Henrik Stenson	Muirfield
2014	Rory McIlroy	-17	271	2	Sergio Garcia, Rickie Fowler	Royal Liverpool
2015	Zach Johnson	-15	273	Play-off	Louis Oosthuizen, Marc Leishman	St Andrews
2016	Henrik Stenson	-20	264	3	Phil Mickelson	Royal Troon
2017	Jordan Spieth	-12	268	3	Matt Kuchar	Royal Birkdale
2018	Francesco Molinari	-8	276	2	Justin Rose, Rory McIlroy, Kevin Kisner, Xander Schauffele	Carnoustie
2019	Shane Lowry	-15	269	6	Tommy Fleetwood	Royal Portrush

Records

Most Victories

6: Harry Vardon, 1896, 1898, 1899, 1903, 1911, 1914
5: James Braid, 1901, 1905, 1906, 1908, 1910; JH Taylor, 1894, 1895, 1900, 1909, 1913; Peter Thomson, 1954, 1955, 1956, 1958, 1965; Tom Watson, 1975, 1977, 1980, 1982, 1983

Most Runner-Up or Joint Runner-Up Finishes

7: Jack Nicklaus, 1964, 1967, 1968, 1972, 1976, 1977, 1979
6: JH Taylor, 1896, 1904, 1905, 1906, 1907, 1914

Oldest Winners

Tom Morris Sr, 1867, 46 years 102 days
Roberto de Vicenzo, 1967, 44 years 92 days
Harry Vardon, 1914, 44 years 41 days
Tom Morris Sr, 1864, 43 years 92 days
Phil Mickelson, 2013, 43 years 35 days
Darren Clarke, 2011, 42 years 337 days
Ernie Els, 2012, 42 years 279 days

Youngest Winners

Tommy Morris Jr, 1868, 17 years 156 days
Tommy Morris Jr, 1869, 18 years 149 days
Tommy Morris Jr, 1870, 19 years 148 days
Willie Auchterlonie, 1893, 21 years 22 days
Tommy Morris Jr, 1872, 21 years 146 days
Seve Ballesteros, 1979, 22 years 103 days

Known Oldest and Youngest Competitors

74 years, 11 months, 24 days: Tom Morris Sr, 1896
74 years, 4 months, 9 days: Gene Sarazen, 1976
14 years, 4 months, 25 days: Tommy Morris Jr, 1865

Largest Margin of Victory

13 strokes, Tom Morris Sr, 1862
12 strokes, Tommy Morris Jr, 1870
11 strokes, Tommy Morris Jr, 1869
8 strokes, JH Taylor, 1900 and 1913; James Braid, 1908; Tiger Woods, 2000

Lowest Winning Total by a Champion

264, Henrik Stenson, Royal Troon, 2016 – 68, 65, 68, 63
267, Greg Norman, Royal St George's, 1993 – 66, 68, 69, 64

268, Tom Watson, Turnberry, 1977 – 68, 70, 65, 65; Nick Price, Turnberry, 1994 – 69, 66, 67, 66; Jordan Spieth, Royal Birkdale, 2017 – 65, 69, 65, 69

Lowest Total in Relation to Par Since 1963

20 under par: Henrik Stenson, 2016 (264)
19 under par: Tiger Woods, St Andrews, 2000 (269)
18 under par: Nick Faldo, St Andrews, 1990 (270); Tiger Woods, Royal Liverpool, 2006 (270)

Lowest Total by a Runner-Up

267: Phil Mickelson, Royal Troon, 2016 – 63, 69, 70, 65
269: Jack Nicklaus, Turnberry, 1977 – 68, 70, 65, 66; Nick Faldo, Royal St George's, 1993 – 69, 63, 70, 67; Jesper Parnevik, Turnberry, 1994 – 68, 66, 68, 67

Lowest Total by an Amateur

277: Jordan Niebrugge, St Andrews, 2015 – 67, 73, 67, 70

Lowest Individual Round

62: Branden Grace, third round, Royal Birkdale, 2017
63: Mark Hayes, second round, Turnberry, 1977; Isao Aoki, third round, Muirfield, 1980; Greg Norman, second round, Turnberry, 1986; Paul Broadhurst, third round, St Andrews, 1990; Jodie Mudd, fourth round, Royal Birkdale, 1991; Nick Faldo, second round, Royal St George's, 1993; Payne Stewart, fourth round, Royal St George's, 1993; Rory McIlroy, first round, St Andrews, 2010; Phil Mickelson, first round, Royal Troon, 2016; Henrik Stenson, fourth round, Royal Troon, 2016; Haotong Li, fourth round, Royal Birkdale, 2017; Shane Lowry, third round, Royal Portrush, 2019

Lowest Individual Round by an Amateur

65: Tom Lewis, first round, Royal St George's, 2011

Lowest First Round

63: Rory McIlroy, St Andrews, 2010; Phil Mickelson, Royal Troon, 2016

Lowest Second Round

63: Mark Hayes, Turnberry, 1977; Greg Norman, Turnberry, 1986; Nick Faldo, Royal St George's, 1993

Lowest Third Round

62: Branden Grace, Royal Birkdale, 2017

Lowest Fourth Round

63: Jodie Mudd, Royal Birkdale, 1991; Payne Stewart, Royal St George's, 1993; Henrik Stenson, Royal Troon, 2016; Haotong Li, Royal Birkdale, 2017

Lowest Score over the First 36 Holes

130: Nick Faldo, Muirfield, 1992 – 66, 64; Brandt Snedeker, Royal Lytham & St Annes, 2012 – 66, 64

Lowest Score over the Middle 36 Holes

130: Fuzzy Zoeller, Turnberry, 1994 – 66, 64; Shane Lowry, Royal Portrush, 2019 – 67, 63

Lowest Score over the Final 36 Holes

130: Tom Watson, Turnberry, 1977 – 65, 65; Ian Baker-Finch, Royal Birkdale, 1991 – 64, 66; Anders Forsbrand, Turnberry, 1994 – 66, 64; Marc Leishman, St Andrews, 2015 – 64, 66

Lowest Score over the First 54 Holes

197: Shane Lowry, Royal Portrush, 2019 – 67, 67, 63
198: Tom Lehman, Royal Lytham & St Annes, 1996 – 67, 67, 64

Lowest Score over the Final 54 Holes

196: Henrik Stenson, Royal Troon, 2016 – 65, 68, 63
199: Nick Price, Turnberry, 1994 – 66, 67, 66

Lowest Score for Nine Holes

28: Denis Durnian, first nine, Royal Birkdale, 1983
29: Tom Haliburton, first nine, Royal Lytham & St Annes, 1963; Peter Thomson, first nine, Royal Lytham & St Annes, 1963; Tony Jacklin, first nine, St Andrews, 1970; Bill Longmuir, first nine, Royal Lytham & St Annes, 1979; David J Russell first nine, Royal Lytham & St Annes, 1988; Ian Baker-Finch, first nine, St Andrews, 1990; Paul Broadhurst, first nine, St Andrews, 1990; Ian Baker-Finch, first nine, Royal Birkdale, 1991; Paul McGinley, first nine, Royal Lytham & St Annes, 1996; Ernie Els, first nine, Muirfield, 2002; Sergio Garcia, first nine, Royal Liverpool, 2006; David Lingmerth, first nine, St Andrews, 2015; Matt Kuchar, first nine, Royal Birkdale, 2017; Branden Grace, first nine, Royal Birkdale, 2017; Ryan Fox, second nine, Royal Portrush, 2019

Most Successive Victories

4: Tommy Morris Jr, 1868-72 *(No Championship in 1871)*
3: Jamie Anderson, 1877-79; Bob Ferguson, 1880-82; Peter Thomson, 1954-56
2: Tom Morris Sr, 1861-62; JH Taylor, 1894-95; Harry Vardon, 1898-99; James Braid, 1905-06; Bobby Jones, 1926-27; Walter Hagen, 1928-29; Bobby Locke, 1949-50; Arnold Palmer, 1961-62; Lee Trevino, 1971-72; Tom Watson, 1982-83; Tiger Woods, 2005-06; Padraig Harrington, 2007-08

Amateurs Who Have Won The Open

3: Bobby Jones, Royal Lytham & St Annes, 1926; St Andrews, 1927; Royal Liverpool, 1930
2: Harold Hilton, Muirfield, 1892; Royal Liverpool, 1897
1: John Ball Jr, Prestwick, 1890

Champions Who Won on Debut

Willie Park Sr, Prestwick, 1860; Tom Kidd, St Andrews, 1873; Mungo Park, Musselburgh, 1874; Jock Hutchison, St Andrews, 1921; Denny Shute, St Andrews, 1933; Ben Hogan, Carnoustie, 1953; Tony Lema, St Andrews, 1964; Tom Watson, Carnoustie, 1975; Ben Curtis, Royal St George's, 2003

Attendance

Year	Total
1960	39,563
1961	21,708
1962	37,098
1963	24,585
1964	35,954
1965	32,927
1966	40,182
1967	29,880
1968	51,819
1969	46,001
1970	81,593
1971	70,076
1972	84,746
1973	78,810
1974	92,796
1975	85,258
1976	92,021
1977	87,615
1978	125,271
1979	134,501
1980	131,610
1981	111,987
1982	133,299
1983	142,892
1984	193,126
1985	141,619
1986	134,261
1987	139,189
1988	191,334
1989	160,639
1990	208,680
1991	189,435
1992	146,427
1993	141,000
1994	128,000
1995	180,000
1996	170,000
1997	176,000
1998	195,100
1999	157,000
2000	239,000
2001	178,000
2002	161,500
2003	183,000
2004	176,000
2005	223,000
2006	230,000
2007	154,000
2008	201,500
2009	123,000
2010	201,000
2011	180,100
2012	181,300
2013	142,036
2014	202,917
2015	237,024
2016	173,134
2017	235,000
2018	172,000
2019	237,750

Greatest Interval Between First and Last Victory

19 years: JH Taylor, 1894-1913
18 years: Harry Vardon, 1896-1914
15 years: Willie Park Sr, 1860-75; Gary Player, 1959-74
14 years: Henry Cotton, 1934-48

Greatest Interval Between Victories

11 years: Henry Cotton, 1937-48 (*No Championship 1940-45*)
10 years: Ernie Els, 2002-12
9 years: Willie Park Sr, 1866-75; Bob Martin, 1876-85; JH Taylor, 1900-09; Gary Player, 1959-68

Champions Who Have Won in Three Separate Decades

Harry Vardon, 1896, 1898 & 1899/1903/1911 & 1914
JH Taylor, 1894 & 1895/1900 & 1909/1913
Gary Player, 1959/1968/1974

Competitors with the Most Top Five Finishes

16: JH Taylor; Jack Nicklaus

Competitors Who Have Recorded the Most Rounds Under Par From 1963

59: Jack Nicklaus
54: Nick Faldo
53: Ernie Els

Competitors with the Most Finishes Under Par From 1963

15: Ernie Els
14: Jack Nicklaus; Nick Faldo
13: Tom Watson

Champions Who Have Led Outright After Every Round

72 hole Championships
Ted Ray, 1912; Bobby Jones, 1927; Gene Sarazen, 1932; Henry Cotton, 1934; Tom Weiskopf, 1973; Tiger Woods, 2005; Rory McIlroy, 2014
36 hole Championships
Willie Park Sr, 1860 and 1866; Tom Morris Sr, 1862 and 1864; Tommy Morris Jr, 1869 and 1870; Mungo Park, 1874; Jamie Anderson, 1879; Bob Ferguson, 1880, 1881, 1882; Willie Fernie, 1883; Jack Simpson, 1884; Hugh Kirkaldy, 1891

Largest Leads Since 1892

After 18 holes:
5 strokes: Sandy Herd, 1896
4 strokes: Harry Vardon, 1902; Jim Barnes, 1925; Christy O'Connor Jr, 1985
After 36 holes:
9 strokes: Henry Cotton, 1934
6 strokes: Abe Mitchell, 1920
After 54 holes:
10 strokes: Henry Cotton, 1934
7 strokes: Harry Vardon, 1903; Tony Lema, 1964
6 strokes: JH Taylor, 1900; James Braid, 1905; James Braid, 1908; Max Faulkner, 1951; Tom Lehman, 1996; Tiger Woods, 2000; Rory McIlroy, 2014

Champions Who Had Four Rounds, Each Better than the One Before

Jack White, Royal St George's, 1904 – 80, 75, 72, 69
James Braid, Muirfield, 1906 – 77, 76, 74, 73
Ben Hogan, Carnoustie, 1953 – 73, 71, 70, 68
Gary Player, Muirfield, 1959 – 75, 71, 70, 68

Same Number of Strokes in Each of the Four Rounds by a Champion

Denny Shute, St Andrews, 1933 – 73, 73, 73, 73 (excluding the play-off)

Best 18-Hole Recovery by a Champion

George Duncan, Deal, 1920. Duncan was 13 strokes behind the leader, Abe Mitchell, after 36 holes and level with him after 54.

Greatest Variation Between Rounds by a Champion

14 strokes: Henry Cotton, 1934, second round 65, fourth round 79
12 strokes: Henry Cotton, 1934, first round 67, fourth round 79
11 strokes: Jack White, 1904, first round 80, fourth round 69; Greg Norman, 1986, first round 74, second round 63; Greg Norman, 1986, second round 63, third round 74
10 strokes: Seve Ballesteros, 1979, second round 65, third round 75

Greatest Variation Between Two Successive Rounds by a Champion

11 strokes: Greg Norman, 1986, first round 74, second round 63; Greg Norman, 1986, second round 63, third round 74
10 strokes: Seve Ballesteros, 1979, second round 65, third round 75

Greatest Comeback by a Champion

After 18 holes
Harry Vardon, 1896, 11 strokes behind the leader
After 36 holes
George Duncan, 1920, 13 strokes behind the leader
After 54 holes
Paul Lawrie, 1999, 10 strokes behind the leader

Champions Who Had Four Rounds Under 70

Greg Norman, Royal St George's, 1993 – 66, 68, 69, 64; Nick Price, Turnberry, 1994 – 69, 66, 67, 66; Tiger Woods, St Andrews, 2000 – 67, 66, 67, 69; Henrik Stenson, Royal Troon, 2016 – 68, 65, 68, 63; Jordan Spieth, Royal Birkdale, 2017 – 65, 69, 65, 69

Competitors Who Failed to Win The Open Despite Having Four Rounds Under 70

Ernie Els, Royal St George's, 1993 – 68, 69, 69, 68; Jesper Parnevik, Turnberry, 1994 – 68, 66, 68, 67; Ernie Els, Royal Troon, 2004 – 69, 69, 68, 68; Rickie Fowler, Royal Liverpool, 2014 – 69, 69, 68, 67

Lowest Final Round by a Champion

63: Henrik Stenson, Royal Troon, 2016
64: Greg Norman, Royal St George's, 1993
65: Tom Watson, Turnberry, 1977; Seve Ballesteros, Royal Lytham & St Annes, 1988; Justin Leonard, Royal Troon, 1997

Worst Round by a Champion Since 1939

78: Fred Daly, third round, Royal Liverpool, 1947
76: Bobby Locke, second round, Royal St George's, 1949; Paul Lawrie, third round, Carnoustie, 1999

Champion with the Worst Finishing Round Since 1939

75: Sam Snead, St Andrews, 1946

Lowest Opening Round by a Champion

65: Louis Oosthuizen, St Andrews, 2010; Jordan Spieth, Royal Birkdale, 2017

Most Open Championship Appearances

46: Gary Player
43: Sandy Lyle
38: Sandy Herd, Jack Nicklaus, Tom Watson
37: Nick Faldo

Most Final Day Appearances Since 1892

32: Jack Nicklaus
31: Sandy Herd
30: JH Taylor
28: Ted Ray
27: Harry Vardon, James Braid, Nick Faldo
26: Peter Thomson, Gary Player, Tom Watson

Most Appearances by a Champion Before His First Victory

19: Darren Clarke, 2011; Phil Mickelson, 2013
15: Nick Price, 1994
14: Sandy Herd, 1902
13: Ted Ray, 1912; Jack White, 1904; Reg Whitcombe, 1938; Mark O'Meara, 1998
11: George Duncan, 1920; Nick Faldo, 1987; Ernie Els, 2002; Stewart Cink, 2009; Zach Johnson, 2015; Henrik Stenson, 2016

The Open Which Provided the Greatest Number of Rounds Under 70 Since 1946

148 rounds, Turnberry, 1994

The Open with the Fewest Rounds Under 70 Since 1946

2 rounds, St Andrews, 1946; Royal Liverpool, 1947; Carnoustie, 1968

Statistically Most Difficult Hole Since 1982

St Andrews, 1984, Par-4 17th, 4.79

Longest Course in Open History

Carnoustie, 2007, 7,421 yards

Number of Times Each Course Has Hosted The Open

St Andrews, 29; Prestwick, 24; Muirfield, 16; Royal St George's, 14; Royal Liverpool, 12; Royal Lytham & St Annes, 11; Royal Birkdale, 10; Royal Troon, 9; Carnoustie, 8; Musselburgh, 6; Turnberry, 4; Royal Cinque Ports, 2; Royal Portrush, 2; Prince's, 1

Increases in Prize Money (£)

Year	Total	First Prize	Year	Total	First Prize	Year	Total	First Prize	Year	Total	First Prize
1860	nil	nil	1890	29.50	13	1966	15,000	2,100	1993	1,000,000	100,000
1863	10	nil	1891	28.50	10	1968	20,000	3,000	1994	1,100,000	110,000
1864	15	6	1892	110	35	1969	30,000	4,250	1995	1,250,000	125,000
1865	20	8	1893	100	30	1970	40,000	5,250	1996	1,400,000	200,000
1866	11	6	1900	125	50	1971	45,000	5,500	1997	1,600,000	250,000
1867	16	7	1910	135	50	1972	50,000	5,500	1998	1,800,000	300,000
1868	12	6	1920	225	75	1975	75,000	7,500	1999	2,000,000	350,000
1872	unknown	8	1927	275	75	1977	100,000	10,000	2000	2,750,000	500,000
1873	unknown	11	1930	400	100	1978	125,000	12,500	2001	3,300,000	600,000
1874	20	8	1931	500	100	1979	155,000	15,000	2002	3,800,000	700,000
1876	27	10	1946	1,000	150	1980	200,000	25,000	2003	3,900,000	700,000
1877	20	8	1949	1,500	300	1982	250,000	32,000	2004	4,000,000	720,000
1878	unknown	8	1951	1,700	300	1983	310,000	40,000	2007	4,200,000	750,000
1879	47	10	1953	2,500	500	1984	451,000	55,000	2010	4,800,000	850,000
1880	unknown	8	1954	3,500	750	1985	530,000	65,000	2011	5,000,000	900,000
1881	21	8	1955	3,750	1,000	1986	600,000	70,000	2013	5,250,000	945,000
1882	47.25	12	1958	4,850	1,000	1987	650,000	75,000	2014	5,400,000	975,000
1883	20	8	1959	5,000	1,000	1988	700,000	80,000	2015	6,300,000	1,150,000
1884	23	8	1960	7,000	1,250	1989	750,000	80,000	2016	6,500,000	1,175,000
1885	35.50	10	1961	8,500	1,400	1990	825,000	85,000	2017	$10,250,000	$1,845,00
1886	20	8	1963	8,500	1,500	1991	900,000	90,000	2018	$10,500,000	$1,890,000
1889	22	8	1965	10,000	1,750	1992	950,000	95,000	2019	$10,750,000	$1,935,000

PHOTOGRAPHY CREDITS

David Cannon – 1, 11 second right, 16, 18, 23, 25 middle, 37 left, 42 right, 49 bottom, 51 bottom, 71, 76 top, 92, 93, 94 bottom, 95 bottom, 96 top

Kevin C. Cox – 2-3, 26, 30 top, 40, 46 (2), 52 bottom, 85, 88 left, 91 bottom, 99 bottom

Tom Dulet – 12 second bottom, 19 bottom, 20 top right

Mike Ehrmann – 4, 10 right, 31 bottom, 36 left, 58 bottom, 70, 87, 88 right

Stuart Franklin – 10 second left, 11 second left, 13, 29 bottom, 31 top, 32 bottom right, 33, 34 top, 35 top, 38 middle, bottom right, 56 top, 57, 68, 69, 72 top, 75 bottom (2), 81, 90 bottom, 94 top

Richard Heathcote – 19 top, 22 bottom, 24 bottom, 25 top, 29 top, 35 bottom, 38 bottom left, 39 bottom, 48, 55 top, 59, 64, 73 middle, 80, 97, 103 bottom

Ross Kinnaird – 11 right, 20 top left, 21, 30 bottom, 32 middle left, 34 bottom, 38 top, 56 bottom, 76 bottom, 77 bottom, 91 top, 101 top

Jan Kruger – 10 left, 24 top, 39 top, 43 top, 47, 50, 51 top, 52 top left, 58 top, 60, 63 top, 66 right, 77 top, 84, 94 top

Matt Lewis – 12 top (2), 20 bottom, 25 bottom, 28 bottom, 49 top, 53 bottom, 55 bottom, 63 bottom, 73 top, 82, 90 top, 99 top

Warren Little – 28 top, 32 bottom left, 52 top right, 62 (2), 66 left, 67 top, 74, 78, 89, 98 top, 102, 106

Charles McQuillan – 14-15, 19 middle, 22 top, 32 top (2)

Francois Nel – 1, 11 left, 36 right, 43 middle, 67 bottom, 75 top left, 98 bottom, 101 bottom

Andrew Redington – 10 second right, 12 bottom, 37 right, 42 left, 44, 53 top, 54, 72 bottom, 73 bottom, 75 top right, 86, 96 bottom, 123 right

Luke Walker – 103 top, 104-105

Historical photos on p.121, 123 copyright Getty Images.

ROYAL PORTRUSH

THE 148TH OPEN

CARD OF THE CHAMPIONSHIP COURSE

Hole	Par	Yards	Hole	Par	Yards
1	4	421	10	4	447
2	5	574	11	4	474
3	3	177	12	5	532
4	4	482	13	3	194
5	4	374	14	4	473
6	3	194	15	4	426
7	5	592	16	3	236
8	4	434	17	4	408
9	4	432	18	4	474
Out	36	3,680	In	35	3,664
			Total	71	7,344